Letters from the Box in the Attic

a Story of Courage, Survival and Love

Barbara Serbinski Sipe

ISBN 978-1-956696-56-1 (paperback)
ISBN 978-1-956696-57-8 (hardcover)
ISBN 978-1-956696-58-5 (digital)

Copyright © 2021 by Barbara Serbinski Sipe

All rights reserved. No part of this publication may be reproduced, distributed, or transmitted in any form or by any means, including photocopying, recording, or other electronic or mechanical methods without the prior written permission of the publisher. For permission requests, solicit the publisher via the address below.

This book is a work of non-fiction. Unless otherwise noted, the author and the publisher make no explicit guarantees as to the accuracy of the information contained in this book and in some cases, names of people and places have been altered to protect their privacy.

The author of this book does not dispense medical advice or prescribe the use of any technique as a form of treatment for physical, emotional, or medical problems without the advice of a physician, either directly or indirectly. The intent of the author is only to offer information of a general nature to help you in your quest for emotional and spiritual well-being. In the event you use any of the information in this book for yourself, which is your constitutional right, the author and the publisher assume no responsibility for your actions.

Rushmore Press LLC
1 800 460 9188
www.rushmorepress.com

Printed in the United States of America

Dedication

My mother, Stanisława Emilia Krasowska Serbinski, is the main reason for this book. A few years after my mom died, I realized I needed to start this project to chronicle her journey through life doing what she felt was right and patriotic. The experience has made me grow in a way that has forever changed my life. There had to have been a subtle vibration coming from the earth after she died to point me in the direction of this project. The book has helped me to value and appreciate my own heritage, and in turn, I give this book to my children as a gift, to aid them in understanding their grandma and valuing their roots. Thank you, Mom, for entrusting me with your precious memories and memorabilia and to make sure that your story is told, even though you never asked me to do so. Through your story, you teach others what you have known, that to be a proud and just person is to be true to yourself. This is an instinctive way of life no matter where you call home.

Acknowledgments

I have many people to thank for finally finishing this project. Since family always comes first, I wish to thank my husband Alan and my three children, Christopher, Stephanie, and Samantha, who were my cheerleaders throughout this process. I wish to thank my daughter Stephanie, specifically, who was not only a cheerleader but was also the one who planted the bug in my ear to tell Grandma's story. I also wish to thank all my other supporters who read my early blogs during the research process and those who recently joined on. They provided unbridled support and acclaim.

Then there is my Polish translator, without whom there would be a mass of letters, handwritten in Polish, I was unable to read. She was enthusiastic and dedicated to helping me decipher the contents of the letters and patient while helping me improve my Polish language skills. I thank Jadwiga Cyparska.

Lastly, I need to thank my brother Andrew. Throughout the process, he was always in my corner with his eternally optimistic approach to life. I am grateful for you and to you, dear Andrew. We are the last of our family of origin—you and me.

Contents

Dedication iii
Acknowledgments v
Introduction ix

Section I- Documents, Letters, Memories

Chapter 1 A Day That Still Haunts 1
Chapter 2 The Will to Live 10
Chapter 3 Dealing with Her Past 13
Chapter 4 The Letters and Documents 19
Chapter 5 Letters from Franek 21
Chapter 6 Back to the Beginning 31
Chapter 7 Outside Forces 37
Chapter 8 Trials of a Conquered Nation 39
Chapter 9 After Only 19 Years as a Free Nation 42
Chapter 10 The Attack That Changed Everything 48
Chapter 11 Fearless Patriots 51
Chapter 12 Russians at the Door 54
Chapter 13 Interrogations - More to the Story 58
Chapter 14 Courage and Survival 66
Chapter 15 The Gulag 77
Chapter 16 The Price of Freedom 82
Chapter 17 Stalin's Reign of Terror 87
Chapter 18 Zdzisław, My Dad 94

Chapter 19 Katyń 97
Chapter 20 Anders' Army 105
Chapter 21 Reaching Freedom 109
Chapter 22 Anemones at the End of Their Journey 112

Section II- Letters

Chapter 23 From Uzbek to the Middle East 121
Chapter 24 The Final Gift 128
Chapter 25 New Lands, New Adventures 132
Chapter 26 The War Was Still Raging 136
Chapter 27 Fighting Back - The Italian Campaign 138
Chapter 28 The Human Toll of War 146
Chapter 29 What was the Polish Army Fighting For? 150
Chapter 30 Fait Accomplis' and its Consequences -
            The Ultimate Betrayal 155
Chapter 31 Poles Scattered All Over the World 164
Chapter 32 Desperate Times 171
Chapter 33 Introspection 174
Chapter 34 The Next Generation 178

Section III- Growing Up Polish

Chapter 35 Another New Land 185
Chapter 36 Making Our Way in the United States 191
Chapter 37 Poland on the World Stage 194
Chapter 38 Living with Trauma 197

Section IV- My Adult Polish Life - Without Mom

Epilogue 211
Conferences 218
Final Thoughts 225
Bibliography 227
About the Author 231

Introduction

Letters from the Box in the Attic was conceived to pay homage to my mother who experienced so much in her young life. This book also pays homage to my dad, but without mom, there would be no story. Because my Polish parents had a love of family, writing this book was not only a way for me to thank them and to recognize their legacy but also to help me understand and appreciate my heritage.

My journey has been a long one, trying to figure out how best to portray their story. The hundreds of letters were very personal and spoke to me as if my mother and father were reading them. Sharing these letters, these unfiltered thoughts and emotions, with the reader is a profound responsibility. This project is a work of nonfiction because there are so many facts, quotes, and photographs that mom saved, including those of people who cannot be identified.

Since I am a history nerd, I believe there is a need to put the past into perspective; therefore, I needed to do factual research surrounding the various events in their lives. It is essential to know the reasons why things happened as they did in order to better understand the dynamics of the past. Because of my love for history, I like to compare the past with the present. There are many parallels from which to draw.

I am the product of a refugee resettlement program because my family came to the United States as Polish refugees in 1951. Since I am an immigrant myself, born in the United Kingdom, living in today's world and hearing all the controversies about foreigners invading, the idea of countries closing their borders to people in need has been difficult for me to process. Society and times have changed over the last seventy-five years since World War II, but family struggles and uncertainty, including parents' desire for a better future for their children have not. This story comes as a result of such a struggle, as my parents' wish to raise two children in a free society required that they never return to their home country. My brother and I were the lucky ones to be given the opportunity to grow up in a free society.

Putting the material together for this book has been an exciting journey, an act of tenacious passion. Having so many letters and documents has helped me put the pieces of my parents' past together like a puzzle, and then to make sense of it all. The fascinating and startling part of my extensive research was incorrectly assuming I knew a great deal about World War II history before I began this project.

Each piece of research has been printed or photocopied; books were purchased and read; countless hours were spent with a translator; many inquiries sent to various foreign government archives, as well as trips to the Hoover Institution at Stanford University and to Warsaw, hoping for additional documentation to fill in timelines and informational gaps. I loved trying to establish a timeline for where my dad was during the war while training in the Middle East based on the dates of his weekend military passes (*przepuski*, in Polish).

The ultimate plum of my research has been traveling to Poland several times to visit newly found family, to Ukraine to visit my mother's childhood hometown, and to find the house where she grew up. During this process, I have met others who are also trying to find information about parents and grandparents from that era through an organization that holds yearly conferences in Warsaw. Those experiences of learning about and talking with survivors of the war have been invaluable.

There have been many books written recently both as non-fiction and historical fiction about survivors of World War II. I am proud to present this piece of nonfiction as a story of survival, courage, and love.

1 Documents, Letters, Memories

Chapter 1

A Day That Still Haunts

It was a Sunday night in mid-February, and there was no answer when I tried to call my mother. We had a ritual each week whereby we took turns calling each other on Sunday evening. Now, it was my turn to call at 10 p.m. Chicago time. Sometimes, mom fell asleep in her living room while watching the news. She lived in Pittsburgh where it was an hour late. I waited and called again. I had an uneasy feeling about not reaching her but dismissed it. "Surely, she is soaking in the tub and didn't hear the phone," I told myself and my daughter, Stephanie. I was definitely concerned after the third failed call but said to Steph, "I'll call again in the morning."

Since that night, I have second-guessed my decision to delay the call a thousand times. I should have tried to contact one of her neighbors that night. On Monday morning, Presidents' Day 2007, I was off from work and making my morning coffee. I tried to call mom again, but still, there was no answer. Sensing something ominous, I called her next-door neighbors, a sweet young couple with three kids who were kind to mom and watched out for her. All I got was their answering machine. I then called the neighbor across the street, and when Mr. Maloney answered the phone, I frantically explained the situation. I asked him if he could ring her doorbell and check on her.

I waited for what seemed like hours for Mr. Maloney to call back. He was an older gentleman who also lived alone because he had lost his wife to a recent illness. I felt fortunate to reach him that morning. Luckily, over the years, the older neighbors had learned to watch out for each other. I was very grateful to have Mr. Maloney there to help. His return call finally came, and the news was not good. It was everything that I had suppressed over the course of the previous night into that morning. He knew she had not yet been outside that morning since the light dusting of snow was still fresh, with no footprints. He found he couldn't get into the house because my mother not only dead-bolted the front door but locked the storm door as well, which was her security habit. He called the police who broke in and found my mother on the kitchen floor in front of the stove. She must have been fixing some tea and had a stroke, but she was still alive. The paramedics were called and she was taken to the hospital, which mercifully, was only half a block away.

I immediately called my boss, told him that I needed to leave for a few days, and got on the first flight out of O'Hare airport. So, there I was at the hospital on Monday, the day she was discovered, waiting for my brother to drive to Pittsburgh from his home in New Jersey. Andrew arrived soon afterward.

The doctors did not expect her to live through the night, news which I found hard to process. Mom had a good and full life since my father died, devoting herself to her family, my brother, and me. Logically, I did understand that she might die. Because of my inaction the night before, the guilt I felt was growing. Had I tried to make contact with a neighbor Sunday night, I could have gotten her care sooner, but I did not want to make a fuss if one wasn't needed. The "what-if" game was beginning.

Mom was on oxygen; her face was swollen to the size of what might have been a basketball. I marveled at the wonders of the human body while looking at her face. How could skin stretch that much? She did not look like our mother but some poor creature who was gasping for breath. We each would hold and stroke her hand, talk to her, saying we were there and how much we loved her.

The diagnosis was that she had suffered a brain bleed, a type of stroke caused by a burst artery and subsequent pooling of blood that puts pressure on the brain tissue, resulting in the death of brain cells. The doctors did not advise surgery. They felt that this particular surgery was dangerous and would not reverse the effects of the stroke. But she took such good care of herself! How could this have happened?

For years, mom had taken blood pressure medication, and even with that, her pressure was often too high. The next morning, a nurse asked about a living will, which mom had never prepared. But she did let us know on various occasions that she did not want heroic measures taken to save her life. There might have been something scribbled on a piece of paper somewhere. The only legal document in place named me as the executor of her estate. This document needed to suffice for medical treatment as well.

That same morning, another question was posed: Should the medical staff provide our mother with any fluids? Of course, I was appalled at the thought of not allowing her something as basic as water! My brother Andy, on the other hand, asked whether fluids fell into the category of "heroic measures." There was not much debate.

She needed fluids to be comfortable, and that was enough for me. She should not have to suffer.

Looking back on that day now and the discussion we had, I see that insisting that mom have fluids was my way of dealing with my guilt about what had happened. I did not want to let go of my mother.

That morning marked the first day of a twenty-seven-month post-stroke journey for my mother, Stanisława Emilia Serbinski, a Polish-born immigrant who, like a cat, seemed to have multiple lives. That day, she embarked on yet another chapter of her life.

As it turned out, because of the brain hemorrhage, mom was left without the use of her left side. Fortunately for her and for us, her speech was not affected, though initially, it was garbled. She was of course disoriented, wondering why she was in the hospital, but as the days went by, she knew she had to get better.

She required speech therapy and, later on, monitoring of her swallowing capabilities. Through it all, mom was determined to recover and do all that was necessary to get to that point. She had heart bypass surgery and a pacemaker implant, as well as battling uterine cancer and recovering after gallbladder surgery. She was very familiar with her medical community because she lived half a block from the hospital and volunteered one day a week in the hospital mailroom. News quickly spread among mom's friends and hospital staff that she had suffered a stroke and had been admitted.

I don't believe that people who are so profoundly ill realize the battle they have on their hands and what it takes to make a significant recovery. Mom was no different. Dutifully, she did what anyone asked as her recovery plan was put together. She confronted the twice-daily physical therapy sessions with enthusiasm and willingly took the different medicines prescribed. Would she ever go home? That question plagued me every time I thought about it. Her beloved house was literally a half-block south of the hospital, but as the weeks of recovery continued, I began to realize that she would never go back to living there alone.

My brother and I tag-teamed our weekend visits to Pittsburgh. The aftereffects of her stroke and lack of progress from physical therapy revealed that mom had a non-functioning left side that prevented her from getting herself up and out of a wheelchair unassisted. Vocational therapy was also a challenge as she tried to get her left arm muscles to fire. In order for her to function on her own again, she would need to use her left hand to grasp objects and to shift her weight when needed. Clearly, her left side was compromised. Therapists concentrated on strengthening her usable right side.

For me, mom's recovery was difficult and perplexing to watch, since the pressure and profound responsibility to make decisions on her behalf were mine. After all, this was my mother and I needed to decide her fate from that point forward. With my brother's help and advice, we rose to the occasion and made these decisions. I have to be one of the luckiest people to have such an understanding and reasonable brother. We have never had a crossword about mom's care. As usual, mom was ecstatic when we visited her, and now, she took much comfort in the fact that both of her children were there to help her through this crisis. With our help, she knew she would go home one day and resume her life, which she was determined to do. As mom saw it, she was strong physically and would recover after a life-threatening event. My view was not as optimistic, however. I was concerned that she was not able to think realistically about her progress, thus I found myself in an emotional quandary. I knew what mom wanted—she wanted to go home! My brother Andy was reacting to what she wanted, while I believed her perception of reality was skewed. The option of her going home to full-time home care was unrealistic, not just for mom but also for us. Her house was not conducive to someone with her needs, and Andrew and I both lived a great distance from Pittsburgh.

My mom had a very engaging personality which endeared her to all the hospital staff who cared for her. The physical therapists and entire nursing staff loved my mom because she always had a joke to tell, a smile on her face, and without fail, cooperated fully, doing everything they asked.

Having been a widow for 27 years with my brother and me living away, she proudly lived alone. Prior to her stroke, she had several health issues, but as she would say, "After all, I'm 87 years old!" She was pleased to be so independent. Quoting her advancing age was her badge of honor which she wore with great pride and satisfaction. She was defiant, fiercely independent, and would not wear a medical alert necklace monitor. Eight months prior, my brother got her a medical alert necklace to wear around the house so she could call for help if she fell or otherwise needed help, but she said it was not necessary. She actually hung it up near the phone and went about her business. After all, she was in her own home where she was safe; it was her attitude. The subscription was canceled at the end of December, two months prior to her stroke.

As Emma grew older, she lost some of her gusto for life, even though she tried to stay active by walking in and around town but admitted many times that she was ready to join her husband in the afterlife. Her mantra was that "It's no fun getting old." She often told the story of having a special insurance policy in place for her old age. The story about the amusing agreement that mom liked to tell was that a friend's husband would back up in his driveway and run over mom as she walked by. But by 2007, her friend's husband had passed away, and eventually, her friend pre-deceased mom.

She was fondly called Emma by her American friends. Her Polish name, Stanisława, was a foreign name to many Americans who could not relate to a woman called Stanley. From Polish to English, the name translates to Stanley since there is no feminine version for Stanisława. It was suitable for a boy, but a girl named "Stanley"? Probably not! Her friends started calling her "Emma," based on Emilia, her beautiful middle name. "Tough cookie" was a good description for this woman, who was both proud and resilient and who did have a fierce will to live no matter how great the challenge and the complaints she could have voiced about her life.

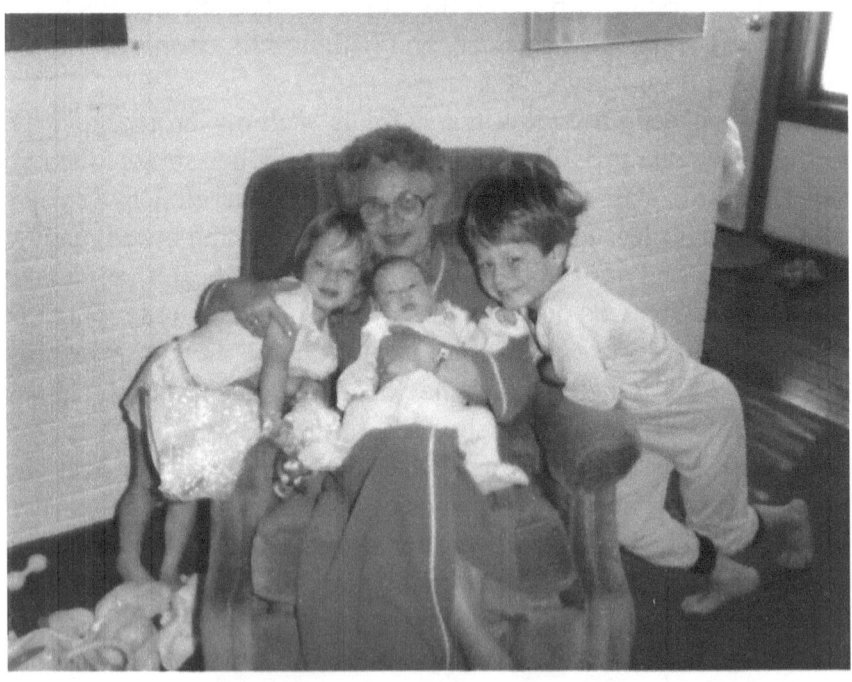

Emma with Grandkids—Stephanie, Samantha, Christopher.

I believe a person is born with certain innate qualities, and Emma was born a survivor and a fighter. My mom fought through rehab until all progress and recovery stopped. Since the stroke affected the use of her left side, she was able to talk and use her strong right hand and leg. This gave mom a false sense of recovery. Not realizing she could not walk, she felt her life was back to normal. As progress diminished, dementia intensified. Although mom showed a few symptoms of forgetfulness before her stroke, after the stroke, her mental condition deteriorated dramatically. Like a thief in the night, dementia took hold, robbing her of any chance to return to pre-stroke days of living on her own. This silent thief robs the brain of its healthy cells, leaving behind an altered perception of reality. As a result, Emma could not understand why she couldn't go home because after all, in her mind, she could walk and take care of herself.

This was a very painful time for me, watching my strong, independent, and beautiful mother become confused and frightened, needing my brother and me to make it "all better." When she was transferred from the hospital to the rehabilitation center, she thought she could walk right out of her entrapment and return home. When I visited her, she would ask, "Can you drop me off at my house on your way home?" or "Just take me across the bridge and I can walk home from there," or "Take me to the bus stop so I can go home." Her home was a tiny two-story with only one bathroom, which was on the second floor. The house would have to be retrofitted for mom to be able to live on the first floor. And because my brother and I both lived so far away, who would monitor her care? Even if we were able to get a caregiver to come in every day, stay the night on occasion, or live at the house, what would happen if that person could not come in one day or would suddenly quit? Those unpredictable situations would be a nightmare to handle.

The decision was made for us when we were told that because mom was no longer making progress in rehab, Medicare would no longer pay for that facility and she would have to be placed in a long-term permanent care arrangement.

My brother and I agreed that it was best for mom to remain in the Pittsburgh area where she had friends who could come to visit, and of course, we would come to visit frequently. The first facility recommended to us had no vacancies. Emma was then evaluated by an assisted living facility in the Pittsburgh area and we were persuaded that it would be a good fit for her. I succumbed to this persuasion because I wanted mom to be as independent as she could be in her situation, trusting that this decision was a good one. After all the person making the evaluation was a professional. This facility was not far from the home of a dear friend of hers. Andy moved some of her furniture and photographs into her room, trying to make her feel at home. This soon turned out to be the worst decision and a nightmare of a situation after only a couple of days following her arrival.

We showed her around to orient her to the new surroundings and explained to her what she should expect; but prior to leaving her for the first time in that new facility, I felt like I was abandoning my child on her first day of school or summer camp. She was clearly frightened and did not understand where she was or what was happening to her. Being left at summer camp is what I can relate to because it was what I experienced as a child. Now, the parent and child roles were reversed.

When I was 12 years old and had never been away from home overnight before, I insisted on going away to summer camp for two weeks. By the end of the first week, I was desperately homesick. I hated everything about camp: the counselors, my bunkmate, the cold weather; everything was making me miserable. I just wanted to go home. After contacting my parents, they drove out to rescue me from that hell hole known as Camp Rosary. The assisted living home was mom's hell hole, her Camp Rosary, from which she needed to be rescued. Emma fell a few times and after each fall had to be transported to the emergency room for evaluation. The home no longer wanted her for liability reasons. My mom was kicked out! It was obvious she needed more care and needed to be close to one of her children.

After much scrambling, we flew mom to Arlington Heights Illinois, my hometown, to live at a long-term care facility that was just minutes from where I worked and lived. She had already been moved several times, and each time, it was a traumatic experience. The disorientation and adjustment to new surroundings took their toll. We needed to make sure this was the last move and as much as we both wanted her to experience a more normal life that was not going to happen. The Lutheran Home provided twenty-four-hour care while she continued to express the need to go home to make sure her house was okay, and of course she needed to have her keys to open the front door.

I felt compelled to visit her every day after work and on weekends. Many times, my husband would come for me or be my surrogate. Her two granddaughters were still living in the area and would come by every once in a while. Because mom was now further west, my brother was further away from her than before, but he and his wife would come for an entire weekend to visit at least once a month. Since she had no one else to come to visit, I was her primary caregiver. The terror in her eyes, which I saw when leaving her in the assisted living facility in Pittsburgh, remained during much of her stay in Arlington Heights. Many times, she was terrified and pleaded for me to stay. When I needed to leave, I was neither prepared to deal with the situation nor immune to how it affected me. I would tense up, wanting to cry and scream. I would panic, not knowing how to react. This was my mother; how could I just abandon her? My heart would break every time we went through the push and pull of her dependency and my guilt for not being there 24/7. That look in my mother's eyes still haunts me today. During various phases of her declining mental state, she would disavow me as her daughter. I was her good girl friend because she viewed herself as a very young woman, so it was not possible for me to be her daughter at my age. The first few times she said this was devastating and it took time, but I learned to roll with the phases and remarks.

Chapter 2

The Will to Live

That will to live, those survival skills, that grit were all a part of my mother's being, the fabric of who she was. The will to live and survive was conceived when she was a young girl and carried through the many chapters of her life. I don't believe a person can be taught these qualities, at least not completely, so hopefully, some have found their way to me. Emma was a strong woman who kept our little family together in the face of many challenges as we made a home in an unknown foreign land, the United States following World War II.

My mom and dad grew up in Poland between the two world wars where they experienced a loving family life and a country that they loved. Their life was then interrupted by hardship and loss brought on by the Second World War. Much of what they experienced as young people shaped who they became.

Who was this woman called Emma? She was my mother, a woman I loved dearly and respected tremendously. She had a guarded zest for life. She was someone who always tried to make lemonade from sour lemons when needed.

Parent-child relationships have an interesting dynamic once the child reaches adulthood. Often, the parent must hold on to the superior role, even though they may need to rely on the child; so, it is not always easy for the adult child to get to know a parent as an adult peer, as a friend.

I did not grow up surrounded by grandparents, aunts, uncles, or cousins, so it was hard for me to get a true understanding of family idiosyncrasies through those family stories of what went on back in the day when my parents were young. I knew I had grandparents and an aunt in Poland on my dad's side, and that mom had an aunt, a couple of uncles, and a few cousins, but these relationships meant nothing to me in the abstract.

Mom, as a child—she is seated in the front row
with her hand on her hip. Photo, circa 1930.

On occasion, my grandmother would write to me in Polish, but as a young child, writing back was difficult. It took a long time and it was not much fun, especially because it was in another language. During my childhood, I would hear some names of relatives repeated again and again, as well as some of my mother's war stories, but it did not give me a sense of family history. Some stories were repeated over and over to the point where I developed a shut-off valve in my child brain. "Oh no, not that story again!" I would think to myself. As an adult, I realized that family history is born from stories heard over and over, from seeing photographs, and from inquiring minds who need to find out more about the whys and hows of events. But back then, I asked a few questions. Today, I believe that mom wanted my life to be that of a normal American child, one that did not impose too many details of the past on me.

There was still no escaping some of these stories, and since I am a first-generation American of Polish descent, they had a profound influence on me. My love of European history, especially World War II era history, turned into an expected passion as I grew older. Probably through osmosis, these repeated stories helped me learn about pre-war Poland; stories of what my mom's childhood was like; about her mother and dad; her Polish patriotism; about the Polish people and what they went through during the war.

Chapter 3

Dealing with Her Past

While mom was living in a nursing home in Illinois, Andy and I decided that it was time to sell her house in Pennsylvania and deal with her possessions that had accumulated over a lifetime. So much of what was in her house proved to be either in disrepair or have no real value. Andy insisted that he did not want anything out of the house. Just about all the artwork in mom's house was from Andy's portfolio from his college days at Pratt Institute in Brooklyn, but he did not want any of it. Knowing this, my daughter Stephanie and I drove to Sewickley Pennsylvania, mom's picturesque town along the Ohio River where I grew up. We pulled a small trailer, ready to figure out what we needed to keep from the house.

Mom was a saver; not to be confused with a hoarder, however. If there was the possibility that something could be reused, she kept it. If there was anything sentimental, she kept it. There was stuff everywhere! Mom's living room was full of newspaper clippings, books, and magazines, pretty much as she had left it the year before. She saved all things that represented family or a connection to her past.

My daughter and I found ourselves looking through everything, piece by piece, and found many old-bound calendars and day timers filled with mom's journaling, her written commentary about her life and life in general, covering every page. She never wasted any piece of paper while writing about this or that. Stephanie and

I spent hours poring over stacks of materials, laughing and crying over what grandma had saved and written.

The journal entries in those day timers included hundreds of anonymous and quotable sayings—sayings believed in or simply aspired to live by, as well as entries telling her World War II story. That story I heard growing up over and over again. I knew she had formally documented her experience two decades earlier, a dictated formal version of her story, which was transcribed. She sent both me and my brother a copy of it in the late 1980s. I put my copy into a drawer for safekeeping, never reading it until much later, because after all, I had heard it in bits and pieces my whole life. What I found that day, going through her belonging, was that her journal entries were in raw form, her rough drafts of the document before dictation. These drafts were unfiltered and priceless.

Stephanie and I continued to look through the photos both loose and in albums, books, and other recently saved memorabilia, deciding what we wanted to bring back with us. We then tackled the kitchen, dining room, and her personal bedroom items and clothes. The kitchen, as small as it was, contained scads of paraphernalia as well, including small appliances, pots, and pans that she had not used in years. Mom had no longer used the old Amana gas oven range, which was original with the house in 1963, the year my parents bought it. She used only one burner and never used the oven for fear of blowing up the house. The rest of her cooking was done in the little microwave or toaster oven, which Andy had given her.

The pantry was very neat and tidy with all of her stocked provisions, primarily from a discount grocer. This ensured that she had more toilet paper and paper towels than any one person needed. The paper goods and other supplies mom had stockpiled could last her months in an underground bomb shelter, along with all the canned goods, crackers, and cookies. She also saved partially used napkins and "to go" containers from restaurants and used them to bring back portions of her lunches out with friends. It was her generation that wasted as well as her experience of starvation during the war that produced such a "waste not, want not" person who would not allow herself to run out of anything essential.

To call her frugal was a good description. I don't think she was capable of throwing anything away which could be reused. It's interesting to observe how family traits are passed along. I am guilty of trying to save stuff as well, needing to think twice about throwing something out just in case I would need it again.

Stephanie laid claim to all of Uncle Andy's artwork, while I decided to keep some of her china pieces and a particular curio cabinet, as well as her old treadle Singer sewing machine. That sewing machine was the lifeblood of mom's sewing business and it gave her many years of use, even after she was given a brand-new machine one year for Christmas. The new machine would break down periodically, but her mending and other sewing for others needed to continue. While the new one was in for repair, she had to go back to using the treadle machine because it was reliable. Stephanie wanted the bench from mom's bedroom, where my dad used to lay out his clothes for the next day at night, and a couple of random side tables. Mom had given me her good jewelry sporadically over the years, so all that was left were costume pieces to be divided among Stephanie, her sister Samantha, me, and Goodwill. The kitchen contents were to go to a rummage sale at the neighbor's church, while clothing, including all of her beloved blazers and jackets, went to the drop box at mom's church. After the house was sold, the remaining contents were to be taken out by an estate sale company, which we paid to do the job.

All of her furniture was original from the time I remember living in that house, which my parents bought on credit. After my dad died, mom spent the rest of her life saving money, working as a re-weaver, which today is the lost art of repairing holes in wool and cotton, primarily from cigarette burns and moths. Every season, mom would say, "Thank goodness for the moths; they keep me in business." She taught herself the art of re-weaving which paid pretty well and her skills were in demand. The cottage business she started was supplemented by her mending and sewing skills.

Frugality is also an art she mastered because of a lifetime of needing to do so. When dad died in 1979, she started with a $10,000 life insurance policy, his meager monthly pension, a car they bought together, which was the only new car they ever owned, and a mortgage on the house. By the mid-1980s, my mother had paid off the house mortgage, the only home she and dad ever owned, paid for any major repairs the house needed, and was able to travel to see her children and grandchildren, but spent little money on herself, nor did she ever buy new furniture. Mom's philosophy was that there is no need to be extravagant on unnecessary things, especially if they still served a purpose. She bought essentials only and otherwise saved every penny, with the goal that she would not burden her children later in life if she needed care. My mom succeeded in meeting her financial goals.

Before Stephanie and I left that weekend, I went up to the attic which had been neatly organized over the years. I was drawn up there, somewhat as an afterthought, because Stephanie and I really needed to get on the road to drive home. Once up there, I felt there was something I needed to find. We stumbled on additional clothes which we added to all the bags ready to give away. I began to open some of the cardboard storage boxes and there they were, the two boxes of precious memorabilia that mom kept! I knew she had saved letters and documents from the war because she would often refer to some of the keepsakes, handwritten letters, documents, medals, photographs, and books. Those two boxes were full of precious items that needed to be in my custody. I could not possibly abandon or discard them. To this day, I can't fathom how I almost left without mom's treasures from her past. They represented who she was. Had I abandoned these boxes, it would have been like throwing away pieces of her life, her youth, her heart, and her soul saved for more than seventy years. In good time, I would explore the contents.

Eventually, I began to grasp the scope of their contents: so many letters, photographs, war medals, patches, and epaulets from uniforms and military documents. Mom even saved the belt from her nursing uniform which she wore on her wedding day. The collection of letters and postcards started with a postmark date of

1941, and a couple of dad's documents dated as far back as 1939. Many of the wartime letters were written by my parents to each other. Other letters exchanged information with his parents and sister during and after the war.

In addition, there were many books and cookbooks—books on ancient Polish towns, a book of Polish Christmas carols, a book listing the names of dead WWII Polish soldiers and where they died—all written in Polish, of course. From all of the books my mom saved, I kept one Polish cookbook as a memento for my collection of cookbooks, as well as the book of Christmas carols. What I realized was that I could not part with any of the old photographs of my mother's family from before the war. These photos show my mom as a child and her parents as young people. Other photos show my dad as a young man before the war, but sadly, none of him as a child. One of my favorites is dad wearing his army uniform and standing next to his horse. My parents had received these old photos from their families after the war ended. Just about everything their families had was destroyed during the war, so receiving these photos must have been a special gift, representing a connection to their past and fond memories of an earlier life—a life not yet touched by tragedy.

Dad in uniform with his horse.

Left with what seemed to be hundreds of letters in one of the boxes, what was I to do with them? There must be a purpose for my keeping these letters that Emma left behind. A big problem was that the letters and documents were all written in Polish, which I could barely read, plus they were all hand-scripted which posed a challenge. I can read rudimentary Polish, but only if it is printed. I struggle with reading the language because I am so slow that I eventually forget what I was reading! The language of the 1930s and 1940s was very formal and much of the vocabulary I do not understand. My mother's handwriting, even in English, was difficult to read. What was I to do with this material? I could donate it to the Polish museum in Chicago, but I needed to know what was in those letters. Therefore, I engaged a translator to help me understand the documents. I needed to put events and attitudes into proper perspective and historical context. This required much historical research. I thought I knew a fair amount about my mother and dad's history, about Poland during World War II, but as I started to do the research, I realized how little I knew.

The research and letters became the foundation for this book, which is a story of what happened to two people who became my parents. It is also a story of what being Polish meant to my mother, and how her experiences shaped who she became. And in the end, this is a story of her daughter, who finally understood what the love of heritage means, what roots are all about, and what it means for her to be Polish.

Chapter 4

The Letters and Documents

I loved my meetings with the translator. This was a woman close to my own age, who immigrated to the United States as an adult, whose father grew up in the eastern part of Poland, north of the area where my parents lived. He too fought for Poland in World War II! She was a fountain of information about customs, language, and military jargon, especially when it came to translating military documents. The best way to be able to have so many of the letters translated efficiently was for her to read them to me. My translator read them in Polish while I took notes in English.

On those mornings, sitting with her in the library and listening to her reading my parents' letters, I felt like a voyeur, spying on my mother's and father's intimate words to one another, as well as hearing my mother speak much like she spoke to me growing up. The difference was that during those war years, she was so young, vulnerable, fragile in many ways, confiding her innermost thoughts to my dad, as he did to her. I would become transformed into that time where I wished I could be a fly on the wall and actually feel, smell, and sense what was really happening. While listening to the dialogue of their conversations, I enjoyed getting to know these two people, not as my parents, but as young adults in love, communicating during a time and in a way that was dangerous and may have threatened their survival. Since the translator read the letters to me in Polish, and since there were words I did not understand, she patiently did much explaining. To my credit, even if there were specific words I did not understand, I knew what she was talking about. This overall experience helped improve my Polish language abilities.

As their story unfolded, it became a fascinating journey not just of history, but of human fear and survival, shaping young lives which evolved through adversity.

Chapter 5

Letters from Franek

My mother had written about her personal war experience, which begin in 1939 and reflected many of the time honored stories I heard growing up. The letters between my father and mother do reveal interesting details of those years, but I start this journey in 1947 after my parents are living in England which also marks a time when they received post-war letters from their families back in Poland. That year was also the first time my parents lived together and started a home together since their wartime wedding.

I found sorting the letters a difficult task. Many were grouped together chronologically while others were out of order. Even when I thought they were sorted by year, a few additional letters appeared that did not belong in that sequence. When my mother was alive and when we called each other on Sunday evenings to catch up, we usually spoke about what was going on with the kids, their schoolwork, sports, or what I was doing, and whether my husband Alan was traveling for work that week. Sometimes, my mom would say that she spent the entire day up in the attic, cleaning this, sorting that, painting, or repairing some falling plaster. But knowing how nostalgic my mom was for her past and how significant that time was in her life, I knew that part of her time up there was spent reading and re-reading those letters. I imagined her looking at all the old photographs from her early childhood or newly married, traveling in post-war Italy or starting life in England, dreaming of what her life would have been like had her circumstances been different. I am convinced that is why the stacks of letters were sometimes out of order.

In 1947, many Poles still did not know what had happened to family members or friends after they were separated during the war. In the winter of 1947, following the end of World War II in Europe which ended a year and a half earlier, my mother and father were both living in England, but given their assignments, still not living together. Both mom and dad were in the Polish Army, the Second Corps,[1] and when the war was over, they remained in Italy until 1946. The Army was then sent to England to demobilize. They were married in 1943 during the war, but in 1947, they still lived apart.

As a New Year's present that January in 1947, she received a crucial letter from her beloved Uncle Franek, a Catholic priest who was resettled in southwestern Poland following the war.

---

[1] Polish Second Corps (*Drugi Korpus Wojska Polskiego*): Victims of Soviet deportations from occupied Poland in 1939-40 had been processed by the NKVD and sent to concentration camps, labour camps, or penal exile in Siberia. [1] The Nazi-Soviet pact of August 1939, effectively ended on 22 June 1941 when the German Wehrmacht invaded the Soviet Union. The release of many thousands of Poles from the Soviet Gulags, following the signing of the Polish-Russian Military Agreement on 14 August 1941, allowed for the creation of a Polish Army on Soviet soil. The commander ultimately chosen to lead the new army, Lieutenant General Władysław Anders, had just been released from the Lubyanka prison in Moscow. This army would grow over the following two years and provide the bulk of the units and troops of the Polish II Corps. The Polish II Corps became a fighting force in 1943 fighting alongside the Allies in all theatres of war. About 115,000 Poles, including women, children, and non-combatants, were eventually released to join Gen. Władysław Anders' army. Anders formed three infantry divisions on Soviet soil. https://www.revolvy.com/topic/Polish%20II%20Corps&item type=topic.

Letters from the Box in the Attic

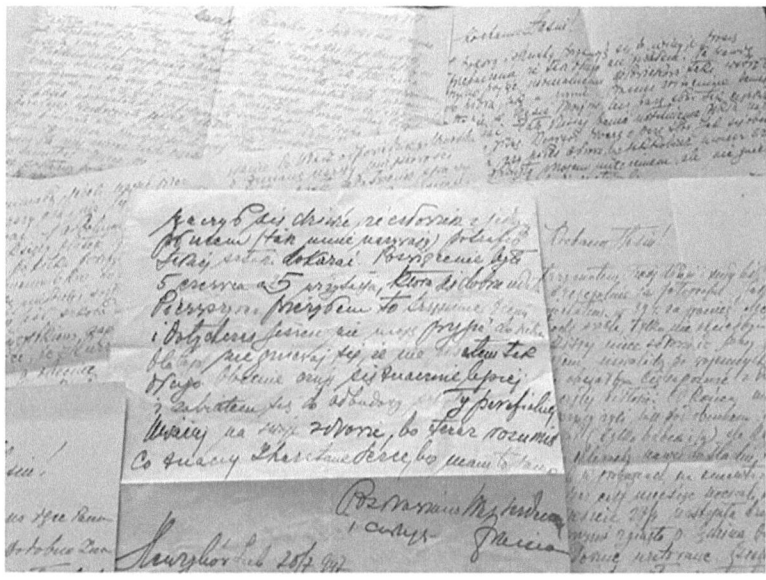

Franek's letters received in the winter of 1947.

My mother, being an only child, was blessed to have many aunts, uncles, cousins, and grandparents in her life, and now her uncle was about to inform her of the whereabouts of her immediate family. Because so many families were unable to find loved ones or even find out what may have happened to them, they relied on help from the International Red Cross, other agencies, and fellow survivors and family members to reunite them or at least learn what became of them.

Wójek Franek (Uncle Franek, in Polish) was my mom's favorite uncle on her mother's side. In 1947, my mother did not know for sure what happened to either one of her parents. Prior to that time, I imagine she agonized about not knowing for sure what became of them after so many years, but she had her theories. Since letters and telegrams were the only way to communicate back then, it is hard for me to imagine relying primarily on the postal service when communication today is so rapid. In the mid-1940s, it may have taken months or years to find out about loved ones.

That first letter from Franek did reveal the fate of her mother from her hometown of Kosów Huculski, in eastern Poland (now Kosiv, Ukraine), including all the details and devastating information. Her mother, my grandmother Magdalena Maria, was dead, shot by Ukrainian Nationalists on March 30, 1944, three years prior. The war involved the Germans and the Allies. So how were the Ukrainians involved? The history of that region is complicated.

Franek spent the war primarily in Kosów, Poland. So much of what happened in this region at the time was complicated by ethnic nationalism, not just by the aggressors who invaded the country. Poland was invaded by the Germans on September 1, 1939, from the west and then by the Soviets from the east on September 17, 1939. The country was then occupied by two aggressors and was essentially split in two. Following a turn of events, twenty-one months later, Hitler invaded the Soviet Union by way of the eastern territory of Poland. That territory would now be occupied by the Nazis, while the Soviets changed their minds and partnered with the Allies. So where do the inhabitants of Ukraine fit into this picture?

It became clear to me after much research that the Ukrainians living in the territory my parents called home was also their home for many prior generations. It is not that Poles and Ukrainians couldn't live together. If one nationality group can have their own country, why would they choose to be ruled by another? The area had been tossed back and forth among rulers over the course of centuries.

Ukrainians were a minority in Poland for over twenty years but they were the majority in my parents' region. They believed the region should be theirs, a part of an independent Ukraine. The area where my parents grew up was known as Stanisławów, a region in southeastern Poland. The region was much like a province or a state. It was inhabited by 69% Ukrainians and 23% Polish. In my mother's town of Kosów, the percentage of Poles was even smaller. While doing this research, I was stunned by the statistics. My mother never spoke of her town in terms of anything other than being populated primarily by ethnic Poles. This fact explains a lot about how she viewed Ukrainian people (not favorably). These people had been her neighbors. She spoke only of growing up in a proud Polish town.

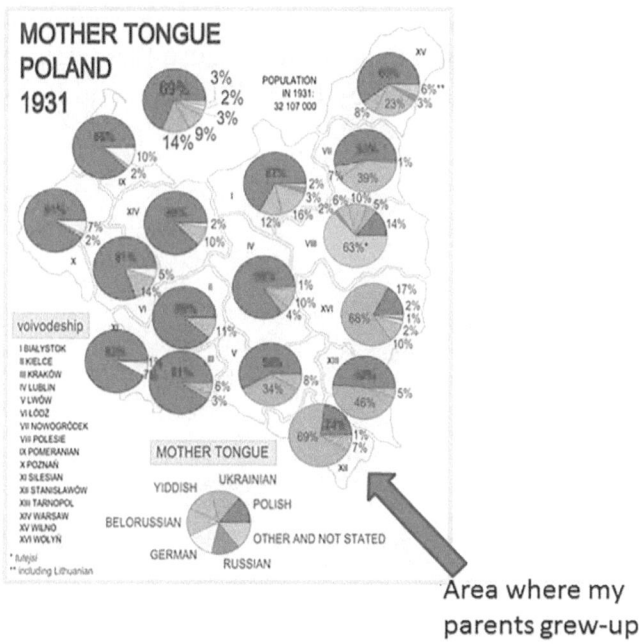

https://commons.wikimedia.org/wiki/File:Mother_tongue_poland_1931_census.png

Map of Poland in 1931—area where my parents grew up—area primarily populated by Ukrainians who declared Ukrainian as their primary language, not Polish.

In order for the story to make sense, some background information is needed. Much of the tension in the area prior to World War II actually started immediately following World War I. Poland received its independence at the end of World War I, while the country's eastern borders were still in dispute. In 1919, border wars ignited the Polish-Ukrainian War and then the Polish-Soviet War. The result was that Poland acquired new land and with it, an expanded region which became known as the Kresy region, or the eastern borderlands. It was the country's frontier, a buffer between Poland and the new Soviet Union following the Russian Revolution, which included the country of Ukrainian that was a part of the Soviet Union. As Poland became an independent nation, forming a Second Republic, the outcome denied the Ukrainian region of the Kresy from becoming an independent country. This fueled conflict among the people because that territory, now ruled by Poland, was inhabited by both Ukrainian and Polish people.

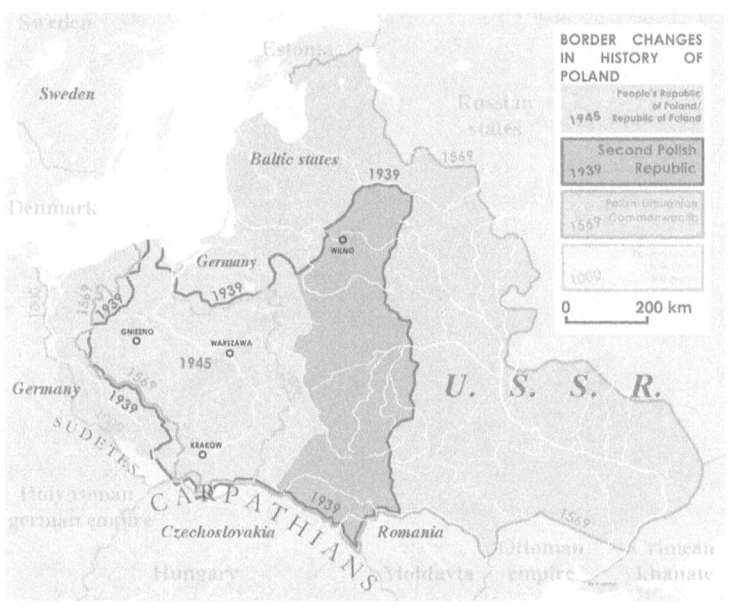

Border Changes Map—Poland through the ages—the main outline depicts Poland's border in 1939 with the darker grey depicting the Kresy region.

Historically, the region was made up of Ukrainians, which made them the majority in most of the southeastern towns of the Kresy with the Poles in the minority. During the 1920s and 1930s, as one nation, there were differing opinions on how to assimilate the Ukrainians into the government and into Polish society. There was government-imposed pacification and repression of the majority who lived in the Kresy region, including the repression of their language, limiting the number of Ukrainian schools as well as to what extent the Ukrainian people could participate in government. As a result, a volatile climate existed, creating hostility against those who were the repressors, the Poles. This unstable environment was exploited when it served a particular purpose during the later years of World War II.

Now that I know why there were tensions, what was in Franek's letter? The letter from Uncle Franek proceeded to explain that he fell gravely ill with pneumonia in January 1944. While his sister, my grandmother Magdalena, cared for him daily, his recovery was slow. By that time, the Nazis were starting to retreat and abandon some of their strongholds with the advance of the Soviet Red Army pushing west. The Soviets were now allies. There were rumors about imminent mass murders of Polish people by Ukrainian Nationalists. The goal of the Ukrainian Nationalists was to claim the territory for themselves, for an independent Ukraine. They were followers of Stepan Bandera, a political activist. If you were a Pole and did not hide or flee the area, you were in danger. During this reign of terror in March and April of 1944, people left their homes before nightfall for fear that they would be killed and their houses set on fire. Because of the simmering fear in the area, Polish residents would hide in the snow at night, hide in the church attic, the town cemeteries, or flee to other towns to escape the prowling Ukrainian Nationalists.

Magdalena refused to flee even though Franek urged her to do so because she had been caring for both her sick brother Franek and their fragile mother, not in her own home but in her uncle's home. Then came the two fatal days in March where close to one hundred people were murdered in Kosów. After caring for her brother, Magdalena was about to return to her own home the evening of March 30, 1944.

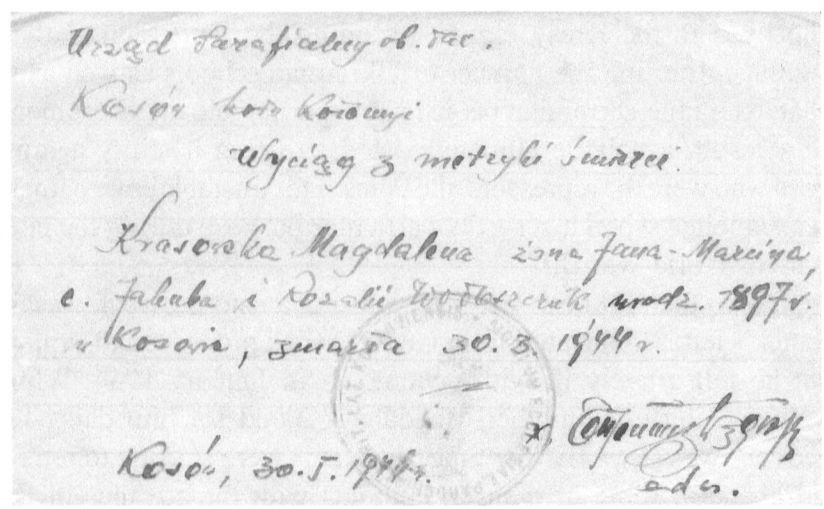

Magdalena's death notice—on a simple piece of paper—
this was the notice mom received in 1947.

Uncle Franek had previously urged her to flee or go into hiding, but she refused. That night, he urged her to go to a home of a Polish partisan for protection, but again, she refused. They argued. That night, Magdalena kissed her mother goodbye, leaving to go to her house, but did not say goodbye to her brother.

Shortly after she left, Franek heard gunshots. Many Poles were shot around the town that night. All this was done to rid the town of more Polish citizens. Many homes were set ablaze, including the home of the Polish partisan who was to provide a safe haven for Franek's sister. Since Franek hoped she had gone to the partisan's house for safety, at first, he feared he had sent his sister into an inferno only to learn the next day what had really happened to her. She had been cornered and encircled by the nationalists who shot her in the chest four times, leaving her body to rot in the snow. Those shots he heard the night before shortly after she had left were the ones that killed his sister, Magdalena.

There was another killing spree in April, identical to the one that occurred the previous month, and the Ukrainian Nationalists were again responsible. They seized the opportunity to control the land they felt was rightly theirs with a display of nationalism which was fueled by the retreating Nazi Army, general lawlessness of the time, and to create chaos for the approaching Soviet Red Army. The Red Army was pushing west from the east to liberate Poland and at that time, many Poles embraced the Soviets as liberators. Magdalena Maria Wołoszczuk Krasowska's body was brought back to Franek's house in a sleigh the next day by some townspeople. She is buried in the Catholic cemetery a few blocks from the house. I was able to visit two large graves in that cemetery, memorializing those who died in the March and April massacres of 1944.

Every time I think of my mother reading these letters in 1947, I feel she had to be dying inside with every word even though she had to believe something tragic had happened to her mother during the war since there was no word from or about her. Mom had sent telegrams to Poland while in Italy trying to find out the fate of her mother but had received no response. This letter of Franek's was one of several letters to my mom that winter into spring. There was a bit of good news in one of the letters. Information had reached Magdalena a few days before her murder that her daughter, my mom, was alive. My grandmother had spent the entire war until that point alone, without her daughter and her husband, who had been arrested and sent to Soviet prisons in 1940. The good news about her daughter must have been a relief following so many years of waiting and wondering.

Additional letters from Uncle Franek revealed that Magdalena had also received news about her husband, Marcin. He actually wrote to his wife in 1941 from Kazakhstan, SSR in the Soviet Union. After that letter, there was no news from him and my mom still did not know her father's fate following their separation, arrest, and conviction in 1940. Since no one knew what happened to him, the only conclusion to imagine was that he must not have survived prison. At least, there was some closure for mom to finally know what happened to her mother, even though I speculate she knew in her heart that both her parents were dead. The mind knows but the soul does not always believe, especially if there is still an ounce of hope for a different outcome. Mom's heart was not the only one that must have been breaking with these letters. I believe Franek, with every stroke of the pen, felt pain and guilt about what happened to his sister while writing this news to his niece.

Chapter 6

Back to the Beginning

So how did my mother get to this place in 1947, living in England and receiving such tragic information about her family? After all, the war started eight years earlier. Much of history reveals the reasons why events occur, but the personal stories, the outcomes of those personal decisions made or those that were made for you, set events in motion and ultimately shape our futures.

While growing up, I learned what made Poland special and why my mother was such a patriot. She loved the area where she grew up. The town of Kosów Huculski, Poland (now Kosiv, Ukraine) was in the southeastern region Poland, known for its hills and beautiful river which was enjoyed by many Poles as a vacation spot. The Huculs, for whom the town was named, were artisan mountain folk who lived in the region and were known for their wood carving, pottery, and tapestry.

Mom fondly remembered her mountain town, and also the Rybnica River which runs through it. Because of its rapids and waterfalls, it was known to be a place for summer tourists. She would say that when she was able to walk in the fresh air, it was a good day.

That thinking transcended to her daily rituals as an adult living in Sewickley, Pennsylvania.

When I spoke to her weekly, she often would say she went for a long walk that day to the waterfall and back because the weather was perfect. The walk to the little waterfall in Sewickley, the town where she spent the majority of her post-war adult life, was her favorite place to walk. We often walked there together when I visited. As children, we would drive there after church on Sundays and play in the creek. Unlike the Rybnica River, Little Sewickley Creek is small. The setting is similar: rustic and serene, hilly and lush with trees which must have drawn my mother's memories back to her time growing up in Kosów. Sometimes, when we took our walks, she would tell stories of her childhood.

After church on Sundays my brother and I would go
to Little Sewickley Creek with our parents.

Kosów was known to have one of the most popular spa/sanatoriums in the nation which was not far from mom's home. Dr. Apolinary Tarnawski founded the spa in 1891 where he pioneered natural healing practices in the fields of physiotherapy and geriatrics. The property is still there in a deteriorated state, which I was able to see on my first visit to Poland/Ukraine. Although he was a trained medical doctor, his spa practiced the healthy philosophy of exercise, fasting, and a vegetarian diet. Many famous interbellum Poles from around the country summered in Kosów and stayed at the spa for relaxation and to receive health care. They were from the country's artistic communities of actors, poets, painters, even university professors and politicians. Between Tarnawski's innovative and natural healing practices in Kosów and the renowned artistic community launched by the Hucul community, Kosów became the Polish Bohemian capital of the area, second to Zacopane, which is in the Tatra Mountains. Growing up in Kosów for mom was a good life.

Her mother's family, as landowners, was financially well-off, which historically meant you were a part of the landed-noble class. The legal privileges of the *Szlachta*, as they were called, were by law abolished by the Second Polish Republic in 1921, but whether the landed people had legal power or not, they still had influence and their land. When mom was a little girl, her parents built a new house in town on land that belonged to her maternal grandfather, which he deeded to them. At that time, much of the town had no electricity, with her street finally getting electrical lines strung in the late 1920s. They must not have had any indoor plumbing either because I remember hearing about how each bedroom in her new home had a chamber pot. These graphic stories about chamber pots were strange for me to hear as a young child. My imagination would go wild thinking about how awful it would be to have to use a chamber pot in the middle of the night or worse to go outside and use an outhouse!

I had repeatedly heard stories of mom and her family going to *Babcia's* or grandmother's house for dinner on Sundays, but the special time was to go there for Christmas Eve supper, called *Wigilia,* where a dinner of twelve courses was prepared and served, representing the twelve apostles. Under the tablecloth was straw, representing the crèche of Christ. An extra place was set for the unexpected guest or traveler, a welcomed stranger, signifying a place for the Lord. These stories I have passed down to my children as a part of our Polish heritage.

Being surrounded by a big loving family was my mother's childhood. Her mother had three brothers and her father had four brothers and a sister. But as an only child, mom found life to be a lonely existence since she had no siblings. This situation gave her the opportunity to develop a special relationship with her dad, whom she idolized because she did not have to share him with another sibling.

As she liked to recall, he was the perfect dad, the one that would get the "Father of the Year" award if there was one. She could always confide in him, tell him all her worries, and feel safe when he held her hand as a little girl. She would say that he had the best shoulder to cry on. And "Oh, he was so talented," she would tell me. "He was a musician, a poet, and good at everything." She obviously worshiped him. At the same time, she spoke differently about her mother, who was the strict one, the one who expected my mom to be a little lady, a little adult, when she was only a small child. Her mother wanted her to be tough, yet have a soft heart.

I find this dynamic interesting. I thought in those days, men in particular were not involved in child-rearing, leaving those chores to the women. Apparently, my grandfather was an anomaly. Many of the early family photos show stern-looking people because the practice was not to smile in photographs, but when I look at photos of mom, and her large family of aunts, uncles, and cousins, I can pick out my grandmother. Her look was as my mom described it, the "no-nonsense" look. At fourteen, my mom was sent off to boarding school in Kołomyja, a town about thirty-five kilometers away, north of Kosów. Since she was only home for holidays and vacations, her time with her dad was even more precious. Many times, I heard my mom say that at any time, even as an adult, she could close her eyes and still feel her father's warm, protective arms around her which felt so good, just like when she was a little girl. Her parents taught her at an early age to be optimistic yet practical. They encouraged her to "hope for the best, plan for the worst, and take what comes with humor and style. Only rarely will anything turn out as badly as you feared. Don't waste time imagining the worst." This was mom's credo in life. She was the eternal optimist.

In 1939, just before the war broke out, my mother had just turned nineteen, had graduated from high school, and had set her sights on attending university; and she met a young man named Zdzislaw who was working in her town. He was twenty-three years old and was special. She felt that her entire future was ahead of her, that a big, beautiful world was to open up. And like most young people, she and her friends were in denial about outside forces interfering with their lives. Nevertheless, there was talk of war. Hitler had already made moves into Eastern Europe by forming a union with Austria followed by annexing the Sudetenland of Czechoslovakia, then taking over the Czech area of Czechoslovakia in early 1939.

After beginning this project and doing Polish research, especially about the Kresy region of which I knew next to nothing, I always wondered why there was such a large Ukrainian influence on Polish land. Having a conversation with my brother Andrew also revealed his surprise to learn that very detail. Yet additional research of the area revealed that the Ukrainians felt it was their land and the Poles were the outsiders. Knowing that my mother only lived in Kosow for 19 years of her life in a region which became Poland around the same time of her birth, she would know nothing different; she knew only that she and her area were Poland.

The bigger picture is what I find interesting. This region had been ruled primarily by the Hapsburg Dynasty/Monarchy (the Austro-Hungarian Empire) as the Kingdom of Galicia since one of the partitions occurred in 1772 until 1920. This area embraced the Austrians, Ruthenians or Ukrainians, and Polish. This triad of ethnic groups had a long history of living side by side. I do remember when mom talked about her dad; she mentioned that in order to preserve Polish history in their region, he would teach

Polish history to children in his basement before the Second Republic was formed prior to 1920 to ensure that the Polish culture prevailed. The official language of the region was German, while in government, the official language was Polish. The minority language was Ukrainian. The conflicts between the Poles and Ukrainians were not new. The bigger picture of historical reality tells me that the area was always in flux. And yes, my mother was of Polish descent, but was it really Polish soil on which she lived? Yes, but only when she lived there. It had been ruled by different countries before and after she knew it.

Chapter 7

Outside Forces

The Sudetenland was particularly important to Hitler because the majority of its citizens were of German descent, and because the Treaty of Versailles that ended World War I took that region away from Germany and gave it to Czechoslovakia. It was Hitler's goal to unite all Germans at any cost, even by defying the treaty. As Hitler postured and threatened, making his intentions known to take the land, all of Europe feared him and wanted to avert war. That year, Neville Chamberlain, Prime Minister of Great Britain, was pleased with himself because he had successfully prevented war by "negotiating" a peace—"***Peace for Our Time***" as he called it. There was no negotiation; the agreement, called the Munich Agreement, simply gave the Sudetenland of Czechoslovakia to Hitler. Chamberlain's quote is remembered best because of the irony. It was ironic that the action of ceding the territory to Hitler to appease him and avert a war for a time simply promoted Hitler's masterplan of taking over Europe.

Austria was next on Hitler's list of nations to conquer. Hitler took over Austria by forcing his will on the Austrian government, planning to unify the two German countries. After invading Austria, he scheduled a mock plebiscite, a vote asking the Austrians if they wanted the Anschluss, or unification, and miraculously, the vote was 99.7% in favor of it! Interestingly, according to the Treaty of Versailles, Germany was forbidden to unite with Austria, the two major powers having lost the first war. But in 1938, there was no leader or country strong enough to enforce the treaty and oppose Hitler.

By March of 1939, there was no opposition, and Hitler knew that any treaties France and Britain had with Czechoslovakia were nullified. German troops marched into Czechoslovakia and took over Bohemia (the Czech portion) without resistance, while Hitler established a protectorate over Slovakia, thus ruling it. It became clear to the West that Hitler was not just interested in a "Greater Germany" since the Czechs and the Slovaks were not German. By the end of March 1939, Neville Chamberlain declared that Britain would defend Poland if it was to be Hitler's next target.

During the summer of 1939, Poland was bordered by Nazi Germany on one side and its perennial aggressor the Soviet Union on the other. As my mother tells the story, her life in Poland at the time was still optimistic, as it is with the young who don't know better. But "the older generation knew better and they were frightened," she said. They had seen it all before, and much too recently. My mother's generation of young adults was patriotic, romantics at heart, who were certain of a quick win and good outcome if there was a conflict, no matter what sacrifices they needed to make. They were prepared to make sacrifices knowing without question that they were going to win. "It would just take time," she said. The country had been preparing and conditioning its citizens for the prospect of war, and the media propaganda was that the Germans were weak and there were no worries because the strong Polish-French-British alliance was in place.[2] That media propaganda may have been a serious exaggeration.

---

[2] Kochanski, Halik - *The Eagle Unbowed, Poland and the Poles in the Second World War*. Harvard University Press, 2012. Page 61

Chapter 8

Trials of a Conquered Nation

Poland was no stranger to aggression from predator nations as witnessed in the 1700s when it was partitioned three times. Poland was previously a country of imperial majesty, spanning the area from the Baltic Sea to the north and almost to the Black Sea to the south. The country began to shrink, and by the late 1700s, the country ceased to exist on the map. Throughout history, the nation made itself vulnerable by allowing the ruling nobility from all parts of the country, each with their own special interests, to have too much power, while at the same time, having no strong central government.

Historically, the Polish people prided themselves on being freedom-loving people; examples of whom were Count Kazimierz Pulaski and General Tadeusz Kościuszko who both fought for American Independence, and both a friend of Thomas Jefferson and the other a friend of Benjamin Franklin. As with these patriots, Poland was a nation that mirrored this love of freedom for life and expression of which was something my mother was extremely proud. However, the government's inability to lead did contribute to the fracturing of the nation in the 18th century. Many good laws were vetoed by factions of nobility because of favored special interests. This resulted in squabbling among aristocratic houses and ultimately created chaos.

The chaos was an open invitation for Poland to be conquered by neighboring nations. The days of Poland's majesty were gone, as it was partitioned three times during the 18th century and eventually disappeared from the map as an autonomous united country. The Polish people remained but under someone else's rule.

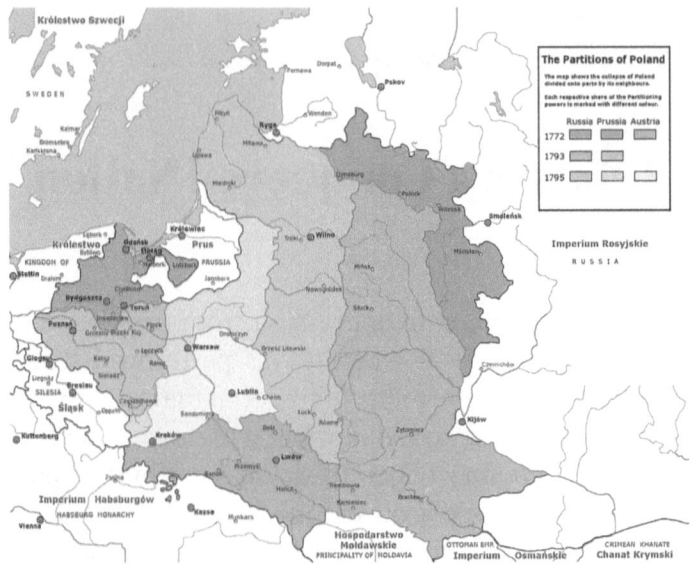

Map of Poland when she was partitioned.

My mother felt very fortunate to grow up in post-World War I Poland, with a newly formed free Poland that emerged after Poland had previously disappeared from the map. Poland had been ruled by three large powers for over one hundred years: the Hapsburg Monarchy of the Austro-Hungarian Empire, the Tsars of Russia, and the German Empire, when Poland reappeared on the map in 1918.

The new Polish Second Republic was established in 1920, with the government lasting just 19 years until Hitler's invasion in 1939. The new Second Republic was not without its internal turmoil. World War I saw Polish brothers fighting each other during the conflict because two of the three previously partitioned areas of Poland were fighting enemies of the third. The Austrians and Germans were a part of the Central Powers, while Russia fought them along with the Allies, Great Britain and France, and eventually the United States. The challenge was to unify the country, while at the same time, try to build and grow an economy that was mostly farm-based, especially in the former Austrian sector, which was where my parents lived. This area where my parents grew up was called Galicia, a part of the former Austro-Hungarian Empire from pre-World War I days. Those lands stretched from Krakow in Poland's southwest to the southeastern portion of what is today western Ukraine. Poland acquired this territory and additional land to the north from border wars with Ukraine in 1919 and with the new Soviet Union in 1920. Today, this land belongs to Belarus and Lithuania to the north and Ukraine to the south.

With Poland emerging as a new nation, the eastern frontier called Kresy needed to become Polonized, while the Ukrainians and the Belarusians needed to be assimilated into Polish society. To make this happen, the government sold parcels of land to Polish families to settle and farm. Some veteran Polish Army officers were given these parcels of land in gratitude for their service during World War I. The southern part of the Kresy, which my parents called home, was heavily populated by Ukrainians from many generations that passed, who did not appreciate settlers coming into their villages. My mother's Polish family lived in the area as well for several generations; the area was tossed back and forth among nations for decades. In 1931, her town of Kosów had only 7.2% of its population claiming Polish was their first language. For whatever reason, my mother never spoke of a divided town or ethnic tensions. Maybe this was because the nation and she, herself, were so young, and because of her love of country, she only saw what was good.

Chapter 9

After Only 19 Years as a Free Nation

When Hitler invaded Poland from the west on September 1, 1939, the Poles fought back unlike Czechoslovakia which offered Hitler no resistance earlier that year. Hitler thought that he could take over Poland easily and did not think that certain alliances and treaties would be honored by the West. Poland had an alliance with both Great Britain and France and the Poles counted on help from the West to defend their nation against Hitler as Neville Chamberlain (UK) had promised. During the early months after Great Britain and France declared war on Germany, the West called the conflict a **Phony War**, because nothing was happening; there had been no defense of Poland, no resistance to Hitler's aggression. The expression is believed to have been coined by a U.S. Senator in September 1939 because of the inactivity on the Western Front.[3]

    This period of history was not kind to Poland. The reluctant French and British did not immediately step in to fight Hitler. Instead of fighting, Europe sat back in its indecision, not wanting to fight and not being ready to fight again. World War I was to be "the war to end all wars." The first battle of any significance was the Battle of France in May 1940, which resulted in the evacuation of British and Allied troops from the shores of France, known as

---

[3] *The Phony War.*
ps://en.m.wikipedia.org/wiki/Phoney War

the Battle of Dunkirk. Had Britain and France acted as the treaties and alliances deemed, some historians claim, Hitler may have backed down.[4] It is easy to speculate.

Even though Great Britain and France had declared war on Germany on September 3, 1939, neither was prepared for war and therefore provided no land or sea defense or any offense for that matter for eight months. As war loomed in the summer of 1939, Poland had one million soldiers, but only half had been mobilized by late August. Poland received tremendous political pressure from France and Britain, who pleaded with Warsaw not to provoke the Germans by fully mobilizing. By then, Poland had assurances, signed agreements with both Britain and France that both countries would come to her defense if attacked. Paris went so far as to say that they would launch an offensive against the Germans "... no later than fifteen days after mobilization." This statement was in a solemnly signed treaty that did not materialize. Hitler invaded from the west with a world class army against a smaller, less sophisticated Polish army, not fully mobilized. Poland and its Second Republic was only 19 years old at that time and had been slowly building a military infrastructure, planning for a defensive war with Germany. It was thought that Hitler would not make his move until a few years later.

As Hitler was about to invade, he stated:

> "The destruction of Poland is our first task. The aim must be not to reach some marked line, but the destruction of manpower. Even if the West goes to war, the destruction of Poland must be our first task. The decision must be immediate because of the time of year. For the purposes of propaganda, give a reason for the outbreak of war. Never mind whether it will be reliable. Nobody asks whether you're telling the truth

---

[4] www.rferl.org/articleprintview Molotov-Ribbentrop: The Night Stalin and Hitler Redrew the Map of Europe

or not if you're a winner. In matters relating to the commencement and conduct of the war, it is not determined by law, but by victory. Be without mercy, be brutal."

Hitler's words were uttered on August 22, 1939, at a conference of senior commanders in Berchtesgaden, on the eve of the signing of the non-aggression pact with Stalin, which outlined how the two dictators would split Poland in half. This secret pact was not one establishing an alliance, but one of non-aggression against each other. It did, however, outline hastily drawn boundaries for Poland that would remain intact for decades. Additional pacts between the two aggressors provided for economic cooperation and support for the war effort. There was much positioning among all the European nations trying to create alliances, non-aggression pacts or agreements for protection, and assurances in case of attack. All of Western Europe tried to prevent the inevitable, a Nazi attack. Hitler and Stalin were doing some posturing with each other as well. What is so interesting to me is that both aggressors had their sights on Poland for years, for both similar and different reasons. After World War I, with Poland becoming an independent nation, the country became a buffer between these two nations. Each country had its expansion aspirations challenged. Hitler's motivation was always to conquer Soviet Russia but Poland stood in the way geographically, and he frequently spoke of his disdain for the Slavs (the Polish were then referred to as "Slavs"). Hitler would refer to Poland as that "unreal creation" of the Treaty of Versailles, while Vyacheslav Molotov, the Soviet Foreign Minister, saw the country as the treaty's "ugly offspring."[5]

Hitler's view of Poland was disdain for the Slavs because he saw the German people as "racially superior." But also to colonize

---

[5] Hitler would refer to Poland as that "unreal creation of the Treaty of Versailles". *Bloodlands*, Timothy Snyder, page 116.

Poland, this would make the Poles, essentially German slaves, would give Germany *Lebensraum* or "living space" for its people.[6]

Hitler's goal had always been for Soviet Russia to serve as Germany's breadbasket and an added source of raw materials. Now the question was how best to accomplish this goal. "If I had the Ural Mountains," he said, "with their incalculable store of treasures and raw materials, Siberia with its vast forests, and Ukraine with its tremendous wheat fields, Germany and the National Socialist leadership would swim in plenty." This was said at a rally in Nuremberg in September 1936.[7]

Initially, Hitler had approached Poland to ally with him, to agree to become a German satellite, have a subordinate partnership, and together, they would attack the Soviet Union. This way, Hitler would have Poland without a fight and use it for his agricultural needs. Poland enjoyed being a peaceful nation and cherished its independence. For the last two decades, Poland was independent after 123 years of foreign rule and repeatedly said "No" to Hitler. The leaders of Poland were not enticed by the potential vassal status. Because Hitler orchestrated a peaceful transition of Czechoslovakia into the Nazi empire, Stalin thought the West would not intervene in Eastern Europe if the Nazis attacked Poland or the Soviet Union.

Stalin always envisioned expanding the Soviet Empire and communism westward right through Poland into central Europe as an area for its industrialization, using the "ugly offspring" reference as a springboard. And since the Soviet Union lost the borderlands, including Poland's Kresy in 1920 as a result of the Polish-Soviet War during the border dispute, there was much interest in getting it back and more. Stalin was cunning in his approach to what he wanted. Stalin calculated, as theorized by some historians, that it was better for him to get the British and the French to fight the Germans than to fight Germany himself. Soviet history interpreted that the Munich Agreement, which sanctioned

---

[6] www.rferl.org/articleprintview Molotov-Ribbentrop: The Night Stalin and Hitler Redrew the Map of Europe.

[7] http://www.hitler.org/speeches/09-12-36.html

the German occupation of Czechoslovakia, made it easy for the Soviets and the Germans to form an alliance.

Thus, in the spring of 1939, through back channels, Stalin proposed to Hitler that they form a relationship if they could get over their ideological differences or at least find tolerable common ground. Their common ground was their mutual aspiration to destroy Poland. This proposal led to the two nations forming an agreement known as the Molotov-Ribbentrop Pact. There was, however, a secret codicil in the pact, a designation of areas of influence for both Nazi Germany and the Soviet Union over certain countries to conquer.

The independent nations of Finland, Estonia, Latvia, Lithuania, Poland, and Romania were all in the Soviet sphere and likely to be taken over. All those countries emerged as independent nations following the end of World War I. They had all emerged after the fall of the Russian Empire and the successful Russian Revolution which created the Soviet Union. With this new pact between Germany and the Soviet Union, the Soviets would take back territory they lost after World War I; part of Poland and the Baltic States, parts of Lithuania, Estonia, Latvia, and parts of Finland. Soviet Russia's goal was to reclaim those lands as Stalin disliked how these countries emerged following the end of World War I. Germany could have the Western part of Poland, all of Czechoslovakia, Austria, and Hungary.

Even after disguising their ideological differences, each knew their interests were self-serving and aimed at returning the Central European map back to the pre-World War I status quo with their own twist on who would own which territories.

This pact drew two hostile leaders and their nations into a dreaded union that would change the course of history once again in the twentieth century. These two unlikely allies were ruled, after all, by equally ambitious dictators who had much in common. Each was brutally ruthless and each used the other to achieve a goal, knowing that theirs was a temporary alliance.

Hitler knew he would wage war on Poland after the Poles refused to join him in the attack on Stalin. But since Poland was an obstacle, it was efficient to position Poland to be attacked from two sides. The Soviet Red Army marched into Poland from the east sixteen days after Hitler's attack. This secret pact specified a new partition to wipe Poland off the map yet again.

Chapter 10

The Attack That Changed Everything

Hitler ordered the attack on Poland, alleging persecution of Germans in Eastern Poland. This excuse accompanied a staged assault on a German Radio station in Gleiwiz, across the border from Poland in Germany on August 31, 1939. Nazi SS troops wearing Polish uniforms staged this deceptive assault to give the world further evidence to justify an invasion of Poland. The Nazi propaganda machine was operating in full force. Dead prisoners in Polish uniforms were left behind as proof that the Nazis were defending their own. This was the rationalization for all the events that followed, which resulted in the beginning of World War II.

On the very next morning, a Friday in late summer, the attack began. The day began as a hot weather day. In fact, all of September was dry and hot. All of Poland prayed for rain because the infamous bad roads of Poland would have been become a swampy mess had it rained, making German tanks unable to pass through, but it did not.

The German ground attack beckoned a new form of modern-day warfare known as *blitzkrieg*. There were no more broad fronts as in previous wars. Now, there were highly mobilized armored columns that shattered Poland from three directions. The second aspect of *blitzkrieg* was the mighty force of the air power from the Luftwaffe, the German Air Force. This new assault tactic left thousands of civilians dead in its wake. Civilians and soldiers alike were pulled into the war.[8]

My parents' hometowns were each in the southeastern part of Poland. In fact, my mother's home was only 10 kilometers from the Romanian border. As my mom remembers, people there did not experience the bombs or the fighting and initial destruction from the Germans. But when the Red Army invaded from the east 16 days later, this area's problems began. Losing control of the country, the Polish government ordered an emergency evacuation of all troops into neutral Romania. Poland never formally surrendered but hostilities ended on October 6, 1939.

Pre-war photos of mom and dad taken sometime in the 1930s.

Since Kosów was so close to the Romanian border and because the Polish army was being squeezed by the two hostiles, the army had to retreat and go south. Thus began the migration of Polish

---

[8] Kochanski, Halik - *The Eagle Unbowed, Poland and the Poles in the Second World War*. Harvard University Press, 2012. Page 61- 62.

soldiers and their government out of Poland through Romania, which was, as a border nation, still neutral and willing to help. Many soldiers were able to cross the border as did the government, traveling through to Paris to create a government in exile. After the fall of France in the summer of 1940, the government was moved to London where it remained for the duration of the war.

The country was independent for only 19 years. In a blink of an eye, Poland was once again divided and ruled by foreign powers.

Chapter 11

Fearless Patriots

Following the immediate and successful evacuation, Romania remained neutral and helped the Polish government by accepting retreating soldiers, but that did not last long. There were those soldiers who were not able to get out because Polish soldiers were being squeezed out of the country by the German and the Soviet armies. A few months post-invasion, the Soviets took up positions along the Romanian border and arrested any Polish military personnel trying to cross, so other means of escape had to be implemented. Patriotic citizens in the area banded together and went underground to help the soldiers and officers cross the border into Romania. The hope was that they would go to France or England and continue to fight the enemy, and many did. If the escaping Polish soldiers were caught, they were either shot on the spot or sent to prisons or to labor camps in Russia and Siberia.

My mother and grandfather were among those patriots, those idealistic romantics who helped soldiers escape. For several months following the outbreak of war, their underground network managed to hide, house, and disguise many such soldiers as adopted uncles and cousins, and when it was safe to get them out of the country, they helped them to the border and hopefully to freedom in the west to fight again.

This was the story I heard all my life, and in fact, my mother documented the story she dictated as a personal accounting of her experience. Yet, after extensive research, I was able to find documentation that there was *more to the story* of what these fierce patriots actually did.

During much of this time following the beginning of the war, my dad, that special young man in mom's life, was working part-time in Kosów, mom's hometown, but primarily in his hometown of Stryj which was further north but still in the same region.

Zdzisław Eugeniusz Serbinski was a reservist soldier in the Polish army. He received military training in an officer cadet program during his high school years and post high school education, training during the summer months as a light artillery specialist. He finished a level of training giving him the rank of Plutonowy Podchorąży in June 1937. This rank is between that of a Corporal and Sergeant and was the equivalent of a platoon leader in the United States Army. This was his path toward becoming an officer. During the summer of 1938, he was released from the Army Reserve but then called up again for additional reservist training in July 1939. He was not mobilized until September 3, 1939, when he was called up to fight with his unit, the 29 Pulk Artilerii Lekkiej (29 p.a.l.), or the 29th Light Artillery Regiment of the 29th Infantry Division of the Grodno Garrison in the northeastern part of the country.

He was called to report to the Wilno (today Vilnius, Lithuania), an installation that was an important garrison and mobilization center. Grodno and Wilno were in close proximity to one another in northeastern Poland. The call to arms came to fight the invading German army in the September campaign of 1939 in defense of Poland, two days after the invasion. Some may say it was not early enough, but the Polish government took advice from the western nations who cautioned against a full mobilization against Hitler.

Dad had been involved with the military since 1932 when he was 16 years old, beginning his military training as did many Polish males during the summers while in high school. After graduating from secondary school, he enrolled in university and studied law. He attended the University of Jan Kazimierz in L'wow, *Uniwersytet Jana Kazimierza* (now L'viv, Ukraine), which is now the University of L'viv, for two years and hoped to graduate in corporate law but never completed his law degree. Instead, he began working as a civil servant for a national insurance company, Polish Public Institute of Mutual Insurance, P.Z.U.W., in their property department in his hometown of Stryj, Poland, now Stryi, Ukraine. He inspected buildings and real estate for disaster insurance, estimating premiums and losses from 1938 to 1939. From time to time, work took him to Kosów Huculski, Poland in the southern part of the province where in February of 1939, he met a young lady, Stanisława.

Chapter 12

Russians at the Door

Evil usually happens under the cover of the darkness. If individuals or families were arrested, disappeared, or deported which happened frequently during the first months of Soviet occupation, they were subjected to banging on the front door in the middle of the night, forcing the families to leave their homes at gunpoint. Bullies and cowards used these tactics under the cover of darkness to intimidate and frighten. This scenario was no different for my mother and her father, my grandfather.

Since the war began, for seven months, my mother and grandfather worked with their underground network. They did what was necessary; they got Polish soldiers out of the country. Their region and town were occupied by the Soviet Red Army of Russians. As mom told it, in the spring of 1940, their network started to crumble. Arrests were more and more frequent, and she and her friends were afraid of their own shadows.

They believed they were on borrowed time, knowing that one day, their sleep would be interrupted by banging on the door. As my mom put it, "When you woke up in your own bed, that meant that you had one more day ahead of you." At her home, the ominous banging came on April 17, 1940, at 1:00 a.m. when they heard, "Otkroite!" (open up!). My mom and her father were arrested by the Soviets and taken away. The charge was conspiracy against Mother Russia, even though they were acting in defense of their country, Poland.

Mom never admitted it, but knowing that she would be arrested soon had to take its toll. She had to be relieved to be arrested, knowing she was "on borrowed time," as she put it. The daily tension of wondering whether "today was the day" had to be frightening. What I have wondered since beginning this project was why my grandmother was never arrested as well. Just living under the same roof with her daughter and husband should have been a reason for her to be under suspicion. Maybe someone vouched for her? Or possibly the Red Army had no evidence of subversive actions on her part.

During that winter and spring of 1940, people in the Soviet-occupied region, which was the Kresy or eastern borderland, were subjected to arrest for many different reasons. Arrests came in waves and affected different social groups each time. The flow of arrests may have been intermittent but nonetheless were constant. This was done to instill fear in the hearts and minds of those who may be outspoken or critical of the new order. How a person fared under this new order depended on the person's ethnic background.

The Soviets were very good at breaking resistance by manipulating ethnic hatred—Jews against Ukrainians; Ukrainians against Poles and Jews. In the pecking order of the repressed, the Poles were at the bottom of the list. The ethnic Pole was the group the Soviets came to conquer and remove. Many who were arrested in the early months were turned in by their neighbors. The Soviets carried out these arrests through the NKVD (later to be the KGB). These Soviet "police" were skilled at turning neighbor against neighbor as well as engaging in bribery. Some Poles would report on what various other Poles were doing, their comings and goings, and whom they were seeing. These tactics were intended to retain social control and inspire constant fear. It worked.

The times were disturbing on many fronts. Not only were there arrests of prominent city and county officials, but also of school teachers, university professors, doctors, and lawyers—all the people in any community who were highly educated and could threaten an aggressor with an agenda. The Soviet agenda was to break down societal structure. The landowners and shopkeepers who were successful in business were the "bourgeois pigs" of the day. They did not subscribe to the concept of shared wealth in a communist society.

The population of the region was made up primarily of the previously disrespected ethnic Ukrainians, so if there was something inequitable about the economic makeup of the area, the NKVD was there to point it out. They encouraged Ukrainians who had been oppressed by the Poles to take over their farms or shops for their own benefit after the owners were arrested. These Ukrainians eventually found out that they still had to pay taxes on the farm or shop just like the previous owners did, but now it was to the Russian government. Demoralizing tactics were also used on the children of Poland. As an introduction to communism, the Soviets tore down crosses, holy pictures, and forbade children to pray or sing Polish songs. If the Soviet police encountered opposition, whether an adult or a child, the person was arrested.

All this was being done to Sovietize the region. A month after the Soviet invasion, Stalin called for "free" elections in the region, and all were required to vote. Since the area which my parents called home was annexed into Western Ukraine SSR, only the approved Ukrainian candidates were on the ballot. One person was slated for each position. This election occurred in October 1939. By the end of November, the newly "elected" Western Ukraine Assembly decreed that all those inhabitants of the region were now Soviet citizens. Anyone resisting this new order was arrested. This also gave the NKVD license to pursue all those who were involved in prewar Polish political parties, accusing them of anti-Soviet activity.

Another way the Soviet new order affected residents of this occupied region was with family deportations. Whether a person was arrested for being a prominent member of a Polish community or was simply targeted, that person was either arrested and tried by a tribunal or was deported to Siberia. The result was somewhat the same in end. I say somewhat because the families who were deported were told to leave their homes and were taken away by train to the interior of the Soviet Union known as Siberia. Those arrested were either shot on the spot or forced to stand trial, imprisoned, then taken away to Siberia. Thousands of targeted families and influential citizens were deported.

Unlike the innocent families who were being uprooted and deported, my mother and grandfather were arrested for crimes against Mother Russia. They stood trial, were imprisoned, and then taken away. After their arrest came the sentencing phase where they had to face the accusations and be punished for their crimes. Once brought to the first prison, mom and her father were separated from each other; men were sent to one area and women to another. Consequently, my mom and her dad did not know each other's fate.

Emma was imprisoned in Stanisławów (today Ivano-Frankivsk, Ukraine), a city that was the governing seat of her province. It is unknown if her father was in the same facility. In that town, she stood trial and was sentenced. She was given a receipt for confiscated jewelry, which included a watch, earrings, and a bracelet. The receipt is dated April 29, 1940. My mom kept this document and tried over the years to preserve it by using scotch tape to hold it together, giving it a yellow color which made it look very fragile. Even though my mom's story states that she was rounded up and arrested on April 17, all the research evidence states that it was April 27, 1939.

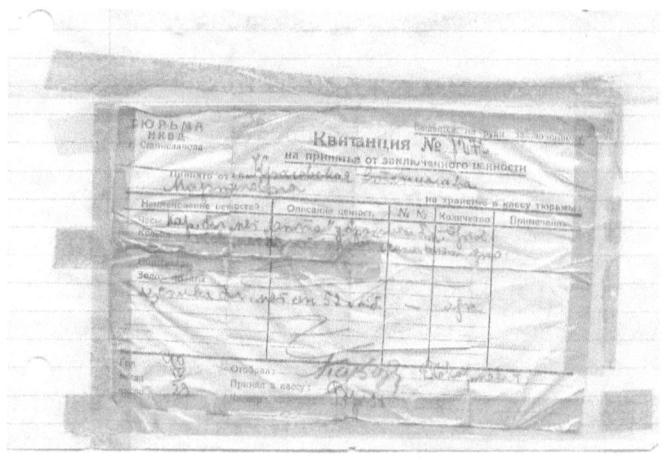

Mom's jewelry receipt

Chapter 13

Interrogations - More to the Story

Mom was forced out of her home because she was a patriot trying to do what she felt was right for her Poland, leaving everything she cherished and loved behind: her mother, her home, her extended family, and her town. My mother, even in the safety of her children years later, still found talking about the experience of being arrested frightening to recall. After the actual arrest and traumatic separation from her father, she recounted her imprisonment which included frequent late-night interrogations to harass and to further frighten her. The immediate goal of her captors was to get signed confessions from the prisoners which might implicate others. These dehumanizing interrogations frequently occurred during the middle of the night when she was not fully awake and terrified. There was an additional purpose to this time of "detention" prior to trial and sentencing.

These "entertaining" exercises, as my mother called them, became a game for the guards. Mom described her interrogator/guard as acting as a "friend" sitting across the desk, saying he wanted to make her comfortable by offering her a cigarette. Then, the games would begin. He asked the same questions over and over, but if the interrogator did not like the answer, if it displeased him, there were consequences. He would come from behind the desk and tell her to sit on the edge of the chair with her legs out straight. From then on, the guard would pace, ask questions, pace and pace some more. If again he did not like the answer, he would stop behind her and pull the chair out from under her. Mom remembered that she never knew which answer would displease him.

Another trick used during interrogations was to have water drip steadily above her head at even intervals. If she tried to avoid it by moving ever so slightly to avoid the drip, her chair was pulled out from under her again. This would go on for hours. In between the various games, the interrogator would yell to the prisoners that "Poland is no longer! The Soviet Union is mighty and Poland with its bourgeois wealth and classes is now off the face of the earth!" This rhetoric of propaganda and intimidating tirades against the Poles were common during the course of the Soviet occupation, especially during interrogations.

As further research revealed, helping soldiers out of the country was not the only activity in which my mother and grandfather were involved. In fact, their interrogations involved other conspiracies. In my own mind, I did question why Polish soldiers were still being evacuated as late as spring of 1940; however, I would not question this since she lived and survived this ordeal.

She and her father were patriots but involved in the "resistance" more than she ever admitted. Through contact with a Polish national archival organization in Warsaw, I was able to get copies of official transcripts and documentation of the activities which led to their arrest and sentencing. These documents clearly state what questions were asked of her during the interrogations as well as the transcript of the trial.

In March 1940, the occupying Soviets and the NKVD began to track the movements of those subversives involved in a secret organization conducting counter-revolutionary activities against Mother Russia. The plot for the Poles in the Stanisławow region was to take back their territory and drive the Soviets out. The interrogation documents revealed certain facts about mom's activities and those of the organization. Having their authority threatened and challenged, the Soviets began to track the movements of members of those suspected organizations. It is documented that Stanisława, my mother, was recruited into a secret organization in February by Eleonore Szydłowska, and took the oath to the organization before its leader Stanisław Guppert. She was recruited to be a document courier between a high-level Polish patriot, Stanisław Guppert in Kołomyja, the town where she attended boarding school, and another patriot in her hometown of Kosów, Stanisław Lachowicz. The school connections she had made it easy for her to travel between those two towns.

One of the interrogations documented that mom knew the wife of Stanisław Guppert, Stefania. Mom would retrieve or deliver items to sew or mend to Stefania's house. As a result, it was easy one day for Lechowicz to ask mom to deliver a package and some papers to Guppert in Kołomyja. When those parcels were delivered, Guppert gave mom another parcel to take back to Lechowicz in Kosów. Since she was registered as a domestic dressmaker, crafter, and mender with the government and knew people in Kołomyja, she continued to work as a courier.

These interrogations themselves were well-documented regarding the date and time they took place. The documented testimony indicated that at first, she denied any wrongdoing, denied that what she was doing was a crime against Soviet authority. She did state that she was just asked to deliver some papers and did not know anything about their contents or the implications of those contents.

Eventually, mom did admit that the local organization leader in Kołomyja specifically asked her to find out how many Soviet troops were stationed in Kosów. She reported back that her contacts in Kosów estimated about 1500 uniformed Soviet soldiers in Kosow. When Polish soldiers were evacuated following the Soviet invasion, their weapons were confiscated at the Romanian border. They were interned for a while by the Romanian authorities and then allowed travel to France.

Since Kosów was in close proximity to Romania, and Romania was still sympathetic to Poland, the secret organization would smuggle arms back to Kosów. These arms would eventually make it into the hands of civilian soldiers to fight the Soviet-occupying army. This was the plan; this was the plot. Whether the organization had any affiliates elsewhere in the region carrying out similar activities in Soviet-occupied Poland is unknown.

My grandfather also played a critical role in this organization. Initially, my mother said she did not know that he was a member; however, she was called out by the interrogator who accused her of not being forthcoming about the information she knew. Now was the time for her to tell all, he encouraged. After further questioning, she admitted that she knew her father was the leader of the local group of five who was under the leader of the secret organization, a man named Lechowicz, while a man named Guppert was the leader of the group in Kołomyja.

She also admitted that this group of five had gathered in her home as they discussed who in town would replace the current Soviet officials, the head of police, and other leaders in Kosow and at the county level. The interrogators told her she needed to turn in other members of the secret group whom she knew. This is when she gave up two names: one of whom was a young woman her own age, Eleanore Szdlowska, who had recruited her. Eleonore was the first who told mom about the secret organization. The other was Danuta Sosnowska who was two years younger than mom when they were in school together. She was the friend who asked mom to attend a meeting at the Lechowicz' home to help them with the subversive plan.

After I retrieved these documents from IPN in Warsaw, Instytut Pamięci Narodowej (Institute of National Remembrance), mom's testimony and documented interrogations from these Polish archives, I was so excited to know what they would reveal, but I was not able to read them because they were written in Russian. Fortunately, my Polish translator could also read and translate Russian. When I returned home from that trip to Poland, she and I met briefly for an overview, but then she took her time and did a critical translation for me to know in more detail what the interrogations and trial summary revealed. At first, I was worried to find out that my mom gave up names of others associated with their organization as a result of the interrogations, which could have resulted in others being arrested. I struggled with how I would feel about the possibility. I came to realize that no matter what they revealed, I was so excited to have further documentation about the interrogations which mom had always talked about.

According to the interrogations, she revealed names of those people who were already arrested prior to her arrest, Guppert and Lechowicz, as well as those who were arrested with her, Eleanore and Stefania. I decided that I did not care whether she did or did not give up any new names to implicate them in the organization.

My mother was courageous to engage in underground activities for her country during war and occupation while experiencing the trauma from the arrest and interrogations. I am very proud of her selflessness and courage. Having digested what she actually did after the start of the war, I asked myself what I would have done in her position. Would I have had the courage to be involved in a plot to protect my family and country? Or the conviction to do what I thought was right, even if it meant opposing a brutal and powerful adversary? Unfortunately, in such a circumstance, we don't know what we would do.

Once she was sentenced for these counter-revolutionary activities, both my mom and grandfather gave their last statements and pleaded for mercy, saying that they were unaware of any crime they were committing against Soviet authority and would never do anything against Soviet authority again. Nevertheless, they were both sentenced to hard labor—my mother to eight years and my grandfather to ten years. Because of the Soviet occupation, all former Polish citizens were forced to become Soviet citizens and as a result of the sentence, they were stripped of their Soviet citizenship, their civil rights for five years, and would have their property confiscated.

Since the men were separated from the women following their arrests, my mom only saw her dad once, on the day they were sentenced. Forty to fifty people from their organization were arrested over the course of several raids that spring, and they all

Letters from the Box in the Attic

stood in trial and were sentenced collectively over three fateful days in September 1940.

The sentencing document was printed in Russian. The translation reads:

In a closed court hearing, the Court Martial of the 12 Army Tribunal, having considered the case against Krasowska, Stanisława, daughter of Marcin, born in the year 1921, according to articles 54-2 and 54-11 of the Criminal Code of the Ukraine SSR. **[NOTE: Her homeland was now incorporated into the Soviet Union which was in the Ukrainian SSR portion.]** *CONDEMNED Krasowska, Stanisława, daughter of Marcin, based on Article 45 and 54-2 of the Criminal Code of the Ukrainian SSR, to correctional - labor camp for the duration of 8 years, confiscation of property belonging to her, and* (illegible) [NOTE: the illegible part must have been the stripping of her citizenship] *for the duration of 5 years.*

Tribunal sentencing document on which her birth year was incorrect.

The criminal code of Ukraine SSR - Article 54-2 charge is for "bourgeois separatism and nationalism; Article 54-11 charge is for being a member of an anti-Soviet organization (i.e. crimes against Mother Russia)." These penal codes were routinely used to charge anybody with crimes allegedly committed against the state. Article 54 paralleled article 58 of the Russian penal code, which was used as a catch-all against Soviet citizens since the Soviet state was established following the Russian Revolution. In fact, in Russian society, it was commonplace to know someone who was arrested and in prison. Prison was the mainstream of Soviet society and imprisonment was a part of the life cycle. The Soviet occupiers would boast that "There are three categories of people in the Soviet Union: those who have been in jail, those who are in jail, and those who will be in jail."[9] This Sovietization tactic was then occurring in the occupied land of Eastern Poland.

Interrogations and the "detentions" served two purposes: the NKVD investigated ties to anti-state organizations and other subversive activities and it also provided a web, tracking people's associations with one another. Forcing the prisoner to implicate another—a friend, an associate, or a family member—was mapping that person's social network.

The Sovietization of that region of Poland was happening from within, not simply being imposed on Polish society as one would think. The new order of Soviet authority exploited ethnic antagonism and personal animosities; thus, creating the perfect storm of neighbor turning on neighbor and turning each other to the Russians because of what they heard, or because of a personal grudge. This was how absolute tyrannical power was becoming established. As my mother lamented, she was tried and sentenced for being a patriotic Polish citizen. Indeed, she was; however, there was no Poland, nor was she its citizen any longer.

Helping to smuggle soldiers out of her country was her official story, and her other nationalistic activities got her arrested,

---

[9] Gross, Jan T. - *Revolution from Abroad: The Soviet Conquest of Poland's Western Ukraine and Western Belorussia.* Princeton University Press, New Jersey.

tried, and sentenced. I wonder why she chose not to reveal the full scope of her courier activities to her family; instead, she stuck to her original story. The extent of her involvement in the secret organization explains why she expressed great fear about returning to Poland after the war. The new set of circumstances explains the trepidation she felt about being rearrested had she gone back. After many decades, this all makes sense now. These new facts are the real story of mom's and her father's true patriotism. Had I not been able to obtain the transcripts of her interrogations and trial testimony, this information would never have been revealed. Too many "war stories" from aging citizens and veterans go to the grave with them, as did this one! I am grateful that I had the opportunity to dig deeper.

On September 23, 1940, my mother saw her father for one last time. She turned around in the courtroom following the trial to look at him, not realizing it would be for the last time. He covered his mouth every time she turned around and she did not know why at first, but it became clear after the judge gave the families five minutes to talk at the end of the trial. She met her father face to face. To her horror, she saw that his teeth had been pulled out. This was a method of torture that was primarily used on the men, as they were subjected to harsher consequences when the interrogators did not like the answers to their questions. Now knowing his level of involvement in the secret organization, the measures taken against him explain the harsh treatment. The methods of torture of the male prisoners were evident as they emerged from their cells with broken arms or legs, while others had scars from burns on their faces as a result of having had their whiskers set afire. I have a question that I have asked myself as an adult knowing the interrogation stories. I have wondered whether my mother, as a twenty-year-old young woman, was sexually abused as a form of consequential torture for giving an incomplete or wrong answer. I have questioned this for a while, but will never know the answer.

On this day of their sentencing, mom must have been wondering if she would ever again see Marcin, her father.

Chapter 14

Courage and Survival

After the trial, Emma and the rest of the prisoners were convinced that they would be sent far into the belly of Soviet Russia and that it would happen soon. There were no more interrogations, so they were no longer on edge at all times and could settle into uninterrupted sleep and some kind of survival routine. The unknown was how much time they had in the Stanisławów prison until they would be shipped elsewhere. Their living quarters were barely humane, with thirty girls in one cell, which was approximately fifteen by fifteen feet square. This is the approximate size of some college dormitory rooms meant to house two or three students. The cell had been their home since they arrived in late April. My mother remembered that there were two or three beds in the cell, so how did they all sleep? As it happened, there was not too much arguing about who would take the beds each night, since there were no mattresses on them. In addition, the cell was a breeding ground for bedbugs, which the girls took pleasure in burning to a crisp with their matches or cigarettes. Many slept on the floor with backpacks as pillows and coats as blankets. Most of the girls were from the same underground organization so they shared bonds of history, the same ideals. They all were in this situation together.

Transportation was a challenge during the war. Each time the Soviets deported groups into Siberia, it took many weeks, and then the train had to return and go to other towns for the same purpose.

Therefore, trains were at a premium. It is thought that her time in prison during that post-sentencing period was due to the lack of transportation to take them elsewhere.

Each day blended into the next while the prisoners waited for a possible transport out of their prison. They still needed to fill the endless hours with some kind of amusement, so they created some sporting events and contests. Since there were fleas and bedbugs in the cell keeping them company, one of the contests involved competing to find out who could catch and kill the most bugs. The winner would get a cube of sugar. The food served was not exactly five-star quality. In the morning, they would get hot water called "kiepiatok" and a slice of brown bread. At noon, it was a cup of mush and kiepiatok. Dinner was worth waiting for because it was a fish soup with floating fish bones and fins as well as floating eyes, which my mom insisted looked back at her. One of the vivid memories I have of mom is one of her hating, absolutely abhorring, fish. After learning why, it all made sense. As long as I have known my mother, a whole fish with its head and eyes intact looking back at her from the plate made her skin crawl. In fact, there were times in restaurants when my husband Alan would order a whole fish and pantomime it "talking" to mom! Neither of us understood how traumatic those memories were of her time in prison. When the talking fish pantomime occurred, it was funny to see her react with disgust, albeit with grace. But in reality, it probably ignited a host of unwanted memories.

While they were imprisoned, mom said that at first, some of the girls refused to eat the food but after a while, she and they realized that if they refused, they would starve to death. Each one of them was determined not to let their captors have that satisfaction. The games continued and the fish soup served more than one purpose. To thicken the soup, the "chef" would add wheat stalks with the outer husk attached, making it impossible to swallow. For added amusement, the prisoners turned dinner into a sporting event to see who could spit the husks from the soup the farthest.

By the fall of 1940, mom and her fellow cellmates were still in the same Stanisławów prison, and still on Polish soil, as they viewed it. They knew Christmas was coming and they promised each other that they would celebrate with some style. When taking their occasional walks outside, they would pick up little twigs and evergreen pieces with the thought of constructing a tiny Christmas tree. Since the trial occurred in September, they were allowed to receive food packages from home which included some decent food items along with some warm clothing. Each of them saved some of their goodies for Christmas Eve supper, *Wigilia* in Polish. As the season approached, the preparations began. From all the twigs, pine, and some thread from green blankets, they created "the prettiest little Christmas tree you ever saw," my mother remembered. Towels were used as a tablecloth which they spread on the floor. One of the girls stood guard in front of the peephole in the door, so the guards would not see their preparation. If they heard the key turn, meaning that a guard was about to enter, they threw a blanket over their supper table.

Once Christmas Eve arrived, the girls were ready for the feast of saved goodies. Even though much of their food was a bit stale by then, it tasted "divine," mom said. They of course had to sing Christmas carols. After all, what would Christmas be without carols to set the mood? In their joy, they forgot to station a person in front of the door and with all the singing and revelry, they were caught.

The guard came in and sent everyone whose lips were moving to solitary confinement. Most of the girls were in their teens, or in their early twenties. This should have been the best years of their lives and, as mom bemoaned, instead, it was one of the most frightening and wearisome. They had no idea what their future would bring, or even if they had a future. Some of the other inmates were older, in their thirties and forties, and were doctors, lawyers, or teachers. As my mom put it, she remembers the women as "pieces of blue in an otherwise stormy and threatening skies." Not all of them had the resiliency of youth and some gave up hope. Others were convinced that all would turn out well and they would one day be freed from the hell of their existence and be able to go home. This hope and unbridled conviction got mom and her friends through those dark days. It would carry them through even darker days to come.

After Christmas and the first of the New Year, during the winter of 1941, the girls were still confined in the Stanisławów prison. Still not knowing when or where they would be moved, they needed to create additional diversions to occupy their time. Thus, they divided their days into sections. One such section included imaginary cooking classes and other home economic interests, where they discussed great recipes, how to properly set a table, color combinations, and flower arranging. Yet another part of the day was devoted to their book club, where they chose a classic that everyone knew and discussed it. This way, they were able to keep their minds occupied and not focus on their miserable reality. In fact, the imaginary cooking classes were so realistic, mom recalls, that the girls could almost taste and smell the food. To me, this would be a torturous experience—being ravenously hungry for only imagining food!

Even though they were isolated in their cell, they found ways to communicate with other prisoners. Not long after a new prisoner was processed, outside information penetrated the thick walls of their hell hole. Because they were able to take periodic walks and could spot new prisoners, through whispers and body language, they gained information from the outside world. During that winter, my mom and her friends were able to learn of their impending fate. The depressing information was what they had been anticipating and fearing; transport into Soviet Russia was in their near future. Even though they were in a hostile environment, they were still on Polish soil as they viewed it. But soon, they would be carted off to the "God-forsaken country," as my mother called it— the Soviet Union.

She remembers a day when a guard came in and said, "собрать' свои вещи и быть' готовыми через полчаса" or "Gather your belongings and be ready in a half-hour." The trucks were waiting for them outside the building and took them to the train station. This brought on feelings of doom, similar to the feelings they experienced months before. Where were they going? What would happen to them now? They felt like "poor sheep going to the slaughter," mom recalls. Again, this "transport raid" was carried out in the middle of the night. The cattle car had a round-bellied stove in the middle with bunk beds on each side and a hole in the floor to be used as a toilet. At least, they were all women on board, but any attempt at modesty while taking care of normal human bodily functions had not been important for quite a while. This trip was reminiscent of the previous one where mom and her fellow conspirators were stuffed together in one cattle car like sardines, but this one would probably take longer. They slept when the train was in motion and woke up when it stopped. They barely got any water during the passage and their only food was dry salty fish. Salty fish is the worst food to eat when there is no water to drink but it makes perfect sense if one is deliberately being inhumane.

My mother does not remember the duration of the trip from Stanisławów prison to the prison in Kharkov, which was in Eastern Ukraine SSR, currently in the Republic of Ukraine, an independent nation. On a contemporary map, the two towns are Ivano-Frankivsk in western Ukraine, formerly Stanisławów, Poland and Kharkov is located in eastern Ukraine. The distance between the two is 653 miles, but in 1941, this distance could have taken two to three or more weeks to travel by train.

Once in Kharkov, they were picked up by trucks, again in the darkness of night, and driven to the prison which was a complex of old buildings with guards perched on all corners high above the prison grounds. The guards were carrying rifles, ready to shoot if needed. Their new accommodation was a cell in the basement of one of the buildings with tiny windows near the ceiling, so it was hard to differentiate day from night. In the corner was a can with two handles, which to everyone's surprise, was their toilet. This cell was even worse than the one they left, only 120 square feet for so many women, and much smaller than their previous accommodation. It was challenging to imagine how they would all sleep in such crowded quarters. The first night, they all collapsed from exhaustion and slept sitting up. The whole travel experience was a blur.

They found themselves in this minuscule environment. They had to figure out how to cope and how to sleep. One very basic credo that they all agreed to was that they had to prove to their captors that their spirits could not be broken. They all promised themselves that "no Russian will ever see us cry." They resumed their daily classes which now grew to include classes in history, geography, poetry, and Latin. At night, since there was not enough space for all to sleep at one time, they divided themselves in half. The first group would sit with their knees to their chins and tell stories and reminisce, while the other half slept. Then, in the middle of the night, they would switch positions. This arrangement worked out fairly well. After all, they had no real choice in the matter. There was a problem even with the best of plans. Even with only half of them sleeping at one time, they were crammed into a very small space, barely able to move a muscle. When sleeping, a person must be able to stretch out. There were a few problems since they only bathed once a week. There was a problem, body odor, specifically smelly feet. Mom remembers that once she finally fell asleep, another person's foot would roll onto her chest and she would awaken from the stench; so, like dominoes, if one person rolled over, then everyone else needed to do so as well. In this miserable situation, there was no one to complain to. As mom pointed out, if you complained, you were sent to solitary confinement.

During her imprisonment in Kharkov, my mother made a remarkable piece of memorabilia. I envision Emma needing to keep herself busy to keep her mind alive. I envision her praying the rosary often, as I knew her to do when she was troubled. Even while living alone in Sewickley, when she could not sleep at night, she told me that she would pray the rosary to soothe herself and fall asleep. Even while in prison, she found a way to make a rosary—from bread. The beads were rolled from crumbs of bread and then strung on a thread from a blanket. At the tip of the rosary was a little metal cross. Mom's dad gave it to her and now it had a dual purpose. She had a full rosary with a cross at the tip for comfort and daily prayers as well as a beautiful reminder of her loving father.

This is both a powerful and fascinating work of art. I remember not only hearing of its existence growing up but actually saw it at one point during my childhood. When I started to go through the box of treasures my mother kept, I could not believe that it was still intact and had not disintegrated after seventy-five years! It is a testament not just to my mother's deep Catholic faith, but to her tenacity and survival instincts. This rosary, I am convinced, got her through the worst of times and it kept alive the hope that she would not only survive this ordeal but that she would see her father and family again.

Rosary made of bread rolled into beads; also a cross from mom's dad.

I also found an amazing autograph book made out of fabric in mom's collection. It reminds me of something a teenage girl would use on vacation to collect signatures of friends or celebrities. It was embroidered with mom's initials, "SK," and below the word "Charkow," and the date, 8/5/41. "Charkow" is the Polish spelling of Kharkov, and the date, written the European way, is May 8,

1941, which coincidentally was my mom's feast day.[10] This may have been a feast day present from her fellow prisoner friends on that day during their captivity. I do wish mom and I could have had the opportunity to study this piece of memorabilia together, so she could have told me more stories.

The outside of the booklet is made of felt material, and the inside pages are made of a sort of muslin, fraying at the edges, with embroidered signatures from her fellow inmates. There are old seam lines on some of the muslin pages that make me think that maybe the fabric was once a pillowcase or a sack of some sort. The book is bound with handmade cording. On the back of the felt cover is an embroidered red heart with an arrow through it. The piece takes my breath away every time I see it, as I try to imagine the circumstances under which this book was made. Her friends may have made it and gave mom this booklet as a feast day gift. Making and signing this piece must have brought them joy during a time of emotional hardship, uncertainty, and anguish. Each time my mother saw this booklet, it must have churned up many memories of those days.

Booklet showing the date of imprisonment.

---

[10] "Feast Day" is in honor of the saint one was named after and in Poland during my parents' time, to celebrate your feast day was more important than celebrating one's birthday.

There was also another item, a hand-embroidered piece from that era that my mom may have made herself. It is a small hand-stitched pouch made of a lightweight burlap fabric. On the front at the top are the dates April 25, 1940 to September 23, 1940, which would be the dates of her imprisonment in the Stanisławów prison; and on the bottom, there is another date, January 17, 1941 to? The January date would be when she arrived in Kharkov, and the question mark would represent not knowing how long she would be there. In between the dates, in the middle of the pouch, there were embroidered words: Bóg - Honor - Ojczyzna, written in a circle, which indicates God - Honor - Fatherland. The red thread was removed at some point. The needle marks on the fabric show which words were embroidered with some of the thread residue left behind. In Polish culture, these three words represented the trinity of thought and ideals in a Polish person's life. To have honor is to express the classic notion of heroism, which is to renounce individualism for the good of the nation (fatherland) and guided by the spirit of a higher power, God - (Bóg), and more specifically for Poles, the Catholic Church. In the center of the triad of ideals is the Polish crest, or coat of arms, which is the white eagle crowned with talons on a red background. On the other side of the pouch in the bottom corner are her initials, an uppercase "K" and a lowercase "s" intertwined, mom's initials. To make the pouch function properly, there is a drawstring around the top to pull it closed.

This is another marvel of craftsmanship because there were no supplies available, only what the prisoners could reuse from their own belongings. I am sure their captors would not have been receptive to requests for embroidery yarn and burlap to supply their craft project needs. They used what they could spare to keep themselves busy for projects which turned into unforgettable pieces of personal history. Not knowing who actually made this for mom, or if she made it herself, it strikes me as fascinating that my mom and her fellow captives were so inspired by their national motto, national identity and patriotism, which brought out their sense of duty and idealism in the face of terror and personal tragedy. However, now knowing the extent of mom's and her co-conspirators' patriotic but subversive activities, it does not come as a surprise that they needed to express their love for their country.

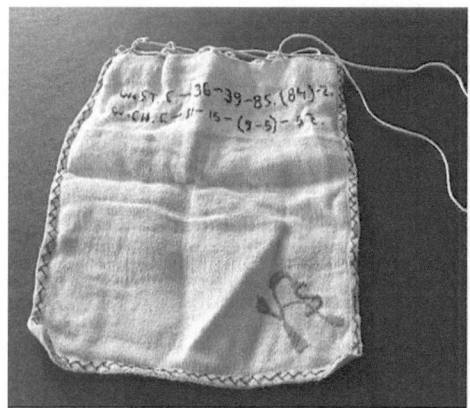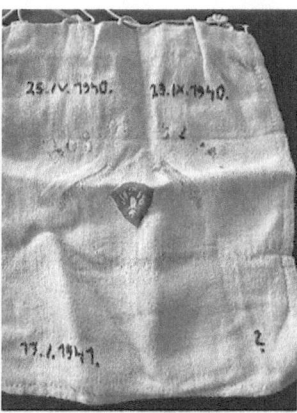

Pouch – made in prison

Pouch—handmade in prison.

During her incarcerations in Stanisławów and Kharkov prisons, my mom received packages from her mother Magdalena. While in Stanisławów, Magdalena would travel 96 kilometers to deliver them herself. Although she was unable to see her daughter, she did get paper receipts for each package she delivered. Uncle Franek mentioned in one of his letters that Magdalena kept those receipts and pieces of correspondence as if they were relics of a saint. Kharkov, which was located in the Eastern part of Ukraine, SSR was too far away for her to travel, so Magdalena sent packages to her daughter and then followed up with a postcard asking if mom received them. Magdalena would send mom salty pork, sugar, and candy and ask if mom knew anything about her dad. One such postcard is among the collection of letters that mom saved. This postcard was written in Ukrainian, since at this time, Kosów was in Soviet Ukraine.

Barbara Serbinski Sipe

Post card from Magdalena dated March 1941.

Chapter 15

The Gulag

Fortunately for the imprisoned, this time, their period of "punishment" only lasted a few months. As they had speculated, their final destination was soon to be known. They would be banished somewhere into the bowels of the Soviet Union. After all, the Poles would be good slave labor for Joseph Stalin and his *kovhozes,* and *sovhozes,* collective and state-run farms, or labor camps, aiding the Soviet economy and war effort. Somewhere in what my mom called the "God-forsaken country" of Kazakhstan SSR, somewhere in central Asia, was their next destination, a gulag,[11] probably their final destination. "Imagine yourself as a speck of dust in the universe," she said. That speck is how mom described herself after being dropped in the middle of nowhere in the Soviet Union. This train ride that found them hundreds of kilometers from northern Iran or from the Urals, the mountains that divide European Russia from Asiatic Soviet Russia, could have taken several weeks to complete. My mom

---

[11] The word Gulag is an acronym of Russian words meaning "Main Administration of Corrective Labor Camps" or "Chief Directorate of Camps." The term was made popular by Aleksandr Solzhenitsyn in 1973 with his book *The Gulag Archipelago*. This was a government agency that controlled the Soviet forced-labor system during the Stalin years. These gulags were first created in 1918, and were used to house petty criminals, political prisoners, as an instrument of repression based on the catch-all Article 58. In March 1940, there were fifty-three Gulag camp directorates and 423 labor colonies in the USSR. http:// en.wikipedia.org/wiki/gulag.

never mentioned where her labor camp was located nor is there any documentation that mentions it. No matter how hard I tried, I could not find out where mom was sent. Allover central Asia, there were hundreds of labor camps, not just for foreign enemies of Mother Russia, but also for their own dissidents, criminals, and their own citizens who fell out of favor with the government of Joseph Stalin. The gulag areas of the Soviet Union are fondly referred to as Siberia. And so there they were, my mother and her friends, not only to be punished according to the sentence that was imposed but to work for the Soviet economy. Many there were hardcore criminals while others were political prisoners who had been imprisoned for twenty years or more. The Poles were not the only privileged people to suffer under Stalin during that time. People from Lithuania, Latvia, and Estonia, the three Baltic States, formerly free like Poland, were victimized by arrests and deportations as were many Jews from those countries. Stalin's reign of terror over his own people and the people of his satellite countries lasted from 1931 until his death in 1953.

Apparently, he thought nothing of killing millions of Soviet citizens and orchestrated a famine in Ukraine SSR in the 1930's where three to five million peasants starved to death.[12] Since he did this to his own people, he certainly had no problem victimizing people of other countries. Now, mom and her fellow prisoners were people without a country. Their native land was occupied by the Soviet Union and Soviet citizenship imposed on them, but as a result of the arrest and sentencing, that citizenship was stripped away. Mom was still a Pole and proud of it.

Emma's gulag experience began in the spring of 1941, sometime in late May or June. Within weeks after their arrival, she and her fellow prisoners heard rumors of Hitler's invasion of Russia, which occurred in June 1941. This information, if true, was great news, they thought. "Let them kill each other and nothing but good can come of it" was the mantra of Emma and

---

[12] Stalin killing his own people. Stanford News http://news.stanford.edu/2010/09/23/naimark-stalin-genocide-092310/

her friends. Their day-to-day life would not change, but with this news, there was a little bit of optimism that made their days easier to endure. Operation Barbarossa had started, which was the name given to Hitler's invasion of the Soviet Union. In actuality, the German invasion of the Soviet Union had more support in the civilian ranks of German Society, because it was never understood why the Fuehrer allied himself with the likes of Stalin. The Soviet Union was for years considered an enemy of Germany. At least now, in 1941, they were fighting the real enemy.[13]

In the Siberian gulag, the camps were not like the traditional prisons of Kharkov or Stanisławów. The accommodations were still wretched but living in a barracks gave them more space. Mom and her friends found themselves literally in the middle of nowhere, many kilometers from any settlement or civilization. There were no more bolted doors, but if a prisoner tried to escape, which a few did, they either died from heat exhaustion or starvation outdoors or came back disoriented and were shot. There were only a few soldiers, the camp administrator, a civilian commissar, and *"the trusted,"* a few trustworthy prisoners who were loyal to the Soviets. Mom said that you might call them "the spies." These few enforcers were all that was needed to keep order. Most of the Russian prisoners were sympathetic to the Polish prisoners, while others were hostile. The sympathetic ones either had selfish reasons for helping the Poles or they had a vendetta against the camp hierarchy. In either case, the help they provided was appreciated and accepted.

Various jobs were assigned around camp and mom's first job was at the stone quarry, which was exhausting work because it included digging and stacking three cubic meters of stones a day. Her diet was a cup of mush and a piece of fatty mutton, but this she got only if she met her daily quota. The Soviets would say, "If you work, you will eat." But this amount of food was not enough nutrition to sustain the needed strength to do such a physically punishing job. Because of the lack of vitamins and the

---

[13] *Berlin at War,* by Roger Moorhouse, page 72

lack of sanitary conditions, prisoners all developed scurvy, which produced large sores all over their bodies that then resulted in infection and high fever. There was no good medical care, so if one got sick, one got sick! Mom said that they all helped each other as best they could, propped each other up either physically or emotionally. They provided each other with shoulders to cry on, only as long as no one was looking, because "No Russian would ever see them cry."

Every prisoner had to meet their daily quota to get the "good" mush and mutton. If one did not make the quota, that prisoner got bread and *kiepiatok*, the hot water. There were many days of starvation which led to a vicious cycle of not meeting quotas and then starving. A few sympathetic Russian prisoners gave mom and her friends some life-changing lessons in proletarian work habits. "Find yourselves a good-sized rock sticking out of the ground. The stones and rocks you dig, arrange them around the big one to form a cubic meter." This was the good and helpful advice they received.

After implementing this advice, they started to meet their quotas so they were able to get food, and then their poor, emaciated bodies were better able to continue the work.

After the stone quarry, mom was assigned to work on the farm, which was considered a "dream job." They felt incredibly lucky! She and her friends met their guardian angel, a Polish gentleman named Stefan Sarvicki from Kavkaz, which is in the southern part of Soviet Russia known as the Caucasus. He was a man in his sixties who had been a political prisoner for twenty years. His family was deported or as the Soviets like to say "resettled" in Russia during the days when the Tsar occupied a part of Poland, during the years Poland was partitioned. History usually has a way of repeating itself. Since Stalin had invaded Poland in 1939, he deported or resettled thousands of entire families out of Poland, as well as political prisoners like my mother, into Siberian slavery just as the Tsars did over the course of the past centuries. For some reason, Stefan was arrested and sent to this labor camp as his punishment. But now, he was the foreman on the farm and as soon as he realized my mother and her fellow prisoners were Polish, he adopted them, helped them improve their physical health, and showed them much kindness. At morning roll call, he made sure they were assigned to his crew. During the day, they were able to eat some of what they picked, as he would look the other way. On other occasions, if they fell short of their quota, he would record it as being met. Even though Stefan was born in Russia, he spoke excellent Polish, knew Polish history, and would occasionally let them read a newspaper to get caught up on the war and political news. He was like a grandfather to them.

During that hot summer of 1941, after Hitler invaded Russia, his recent ally Stalin feared he may lose the war. Operation Barbarossa was initially very successful for Hitler. Stalin's Red Army had been stretched thin especially after he invaded Finland earlier that year, so Stalin needed reinforcements to help fight the Germans. Knowing Stalin's situation, the Polish General Władysław Sikorski of the Polish government exiled in London, began discussions with Stalin, and ultimately persuaded him to allow the deported and imprisoned Polish people as well as POWs to be released from captivity. With Stalin's permission, they would organize themselves as an army on Russian soil to help fight Hitler. The release agreement, known as the Sikorski-Mayski Agreement, was signed at the end of July 1941 and has been referred to as "amnesty" for the Poles. This ironic term, amnesty, suggests that a crime was committed that needed forgiveness. The only crime committed was *against* the Polish people, not *by* them. The official date of amnesty was August 12, 1941.

Chapter 16

The Price of Freedom

"We were more hungry than when we were in prison. The bread was gone, the money was almost gone."

It seemed to my mother that their camp was the last to get official word about the amnesty agreement that had been signed. The Soviet directive from Moscow was that all Poles were to be released. Some camp commandants either ignored or postponed compliance. All released prisoners needed travel documents, which in some cases, were withheld. I have no date for mom's release and, oddly, she did not keep her release papers. But their reality was that they were freed, receiving a new t-shirt and jacket, twenty rubles, a kilo of bread, discharge papers, and a hug from Stefan Sarvitski, their savior. Their gleeful joy had to be tempered with fear and anxiety since all they had known for two years was imprisonment and abuse. What was to be their immediate future? What does a "speck of dust" do in the middle of nowhere when left to find its way?

The Sikorski-Mayski agreement (the amnesty agreement), signed on July 30, 1941, between the Polish Government-in-exile and the Soviet Ambassador to the United Kingdom, gave my mother and her colleagues their freedom, but now they had to find their way to one of the recruitment locations where the

Polish Army was to be formed on Soviet soil. There were so many questions. Where were they? And where were they supposed to go? Where was the safety of their fellow Poles? They knew they had to go south to find one of the collection/recruitment areas, and after their day-to-day hardships of illness and starvation, they had to succeed. And so, they set off on yet another journey traveling by mule carts, trains, but mostly on foot. Traveling through Siberia out of the gulag, going south, meant that they were still in the Soviet Union, but what kept them focused was the need to get to where the Polish delegation was recruiting for the Army. The official delegation, which was scattered around the southern areas of the Soviet Union, was made up of consular officials and *Mężczyźni Zaufania* (Men of Trust). These men fanned out to all the major railway junctions and cities in Russia and Siberia to help the travelers find their way. A total of 20 such Soviet areas were covered. The embassy delegates found that the number of released prisoners who were showing up was far smaller than anticipated. These officials represented both the Republic of Poland and the Soviet Union and were charged with the material and social welfare of released Poles. Diplomatic relations between the Polish Government in Exile and Moscow officially resumed following the amnesty agreement.

In the face of all adversity, my mother was extremely fortunate on several points. She was released from the Kharkov prison just in time not to be murdered. She never mentioned this point even if she had connected the dots. In 1941, after Hitler invaded the Soviet-occupied territory, the Soviets started their retreat. Consequently, whenever they could, before the Nazi advance, the Soviets simply killed as many of their prisoners as they could. Had her release from the Ukrainian prison been delayed by a month, she may not have lived to talk about her ordeal. The other fortunate detail is that her labor camp commandant, once she was in the gulag system, did release his Polish slaves. She could have been in a camp where news did not filter in or the directive to release the prisoners was ignored. As it turns out, hundreds of thousands of deportees did not know about "amnesty" while others who were sick or elderly chose not to make the odyssey out of their imprisonment. Another deterrent to a successful release was that some prisoners encountered problems during their travels where they became stranded in unknown locations. Trains were diverted or returned to where they came from in an attempt to sabotage the former deportees' passage. This was done to keep the people desperate so they would continue to work, and once stranded, they were without food and money; consequently, many had to continue working on the farms. This fortunately did not happen to mom.

The goal for mom and her friends was to get to Bukhara, Samarkand, or Tashkent in Uzbekistan SSR, which was quite a journey. "We were hungrier than when we were in prison," mom recounted. "The bread was gone, the money was almost gone," my mother vividly remembered. They drank water from irrigation ditches and picked crumbs from cattle feed at train stations. They were free at last but barely alive. This was the price of freedom in the Soviet Union.

Along the way, they would meet fellow countrymen traveling in the same direction for the same purpose, having experienced similar hardships. They compared news and would ask the standard questions about knowing the whereabouts of family members, relatives, and friends. So many people were separated from fathers, mothers, husbands, brothers, and children while scattered throughout the Soviet Union. Because of the county's vastness, the scattering of friends and relatives would be like blowing an over-bloomed dandelion into the countryside. The seeds scatter everywhere with some growing into healthy new weeds, while others die. How would you know who would survive and who would not? The will to live was strong for some, like my mother.

My mother's standard question for anyone she met was whether they knew anything of her father's whereabouts. The answer was always "No."

The nomads sorted through all the information that was shared, decided which road to take next, and together, they continued their journey. They believed that there was strength in numbers and the idea of traveling in a group made the women feel safer and more comfortable while trusting each other to find their way.

From September 1939 through June 1941, roughly 1.7 million Poles were either deported, arrested, or captured by the Soviets during the invasion and occupation. These people were herded like cattle out of their homes and forced to leave their homeland to which only a few would ever return. An estimated 760,000 Poles died on the way to exile. Of that number, most were children and the elderly. The children were the innocents of society, the hope of a future Poland, while the many grandmothers and grandfathers were the anchors of the past who had the wisdom and knowledge of life. During the transport to their new country, bodies of those who died en route were thrown off trains between stops without sacred burials. There was no time to dig a grave, say a prayer, or even know where to find the loved one whose body had been left behind. Many suffered during the initial transport, and once they arrived in Kazakhstan, the suffering continued. Even after arriving at their new destination, some deportees were forced to walk in sub-zero temperatures in deep snow, causing frostbite and death. The living conditions proved to be nothing like their homes in Poland. There was no comfort of home, but only a one- or two-room thatched huts with dirt floors which they shared with local families. Many Polish families and individuals continued to live there for decades for various reasons.

Countless of those exiled did not survive their deportations—either the passage to exile, while there, or out of exile after amnesty. It is estimated that almost half of the people sent to Siberia died by the time amnesty was signed and that figure includes those who perished trying to leave the Soviet Union. The devastation of Polish humanity had no boundaries. Countless soldiers who fought for Poland in the September campaign and local leaders, who were rounded up right after the invasion, were brutally victimized by the

Soviets. Over 25,000 Army officers, reservists, political leaders, intellectuals, and government officials were executed in the spring of 1940 on Soviet soil. Of those murdered, 14,000 were Polish career army officers.

Chapter 17

Stalin's Reign of Terror

The Soviet Union had never declared war on Poland but simply invaded. With no declaration of war, the justification for their invasion was to liberate their fellow ethnic Russians living in Western Belarus and Western Ukraine, to liberate them from the brutal Polish feudal lords. All this was carefully planned with the signing of the Ribbentrop-Molotov Alliance in August 1939. Stalin let Hitler do the initial invasion, putting space between the inevitable Hitler invasion of Soviet Russia twenty-one months later, which was anticipated. However, the timing was not. With no declaration of war against Poland, the Soviets did not consider the captured Polish military as prisoners of war but referred to them as rebels and enemies of the new Soviet government in Western Ukraine and Western Belarus.

This newly liberated land was the former Kresy region of Poland which the Soviets lost two decades earlier but now successfully occupied. In addition, the Soviets had not signed the Geneva Convention on the treatment of prisoners governing the rules of war; thus, Polish prisoners were denied legal status.

The reign of terror by the NKVD, the Soviet Secret Police, was the beginning of the Sovietization of Kresy, the borderlands taken by Soviet Russia. Between 1939 and 1941, over a million Polish citizens were forcefully deported to the Soviet Union. 200,000–300,000 Soviet citizens arrived in the Eastern borderlands of Poland to resettle in the vacant homes the deportations created, as Sovietization was the focus.

There were four major deportations of Polish citizens out of Poland and into the Soviet Union's Siberia. The first wave of arrests was of local politicians, government officials, and the settlers who were given the land to farm and raise their families back in 1920. The settlers were those Polish army officers who were given parcels of land to farm and settle in the Kresy region, land given to by the Polish government so these families could start a new life. This gift of land was in thanks for their service to their country following the Polish-Russian border war of 1919. This first group of arrested and deported included any active Polish soldier captured in the area following the invasion and those trying to escape out of the country to the west. These totals were estimated at over 100,000 people.

The first official round-up of families, however, did not occur until February 10, 1940, and it involved many of the families of those soldier-settlers previously arrested, along with middle-class shop and business owners and their families, making up a total of over 220,000 people. Since this region was now, according to the Soviet Union, a part of mother Russia, anyone refusing to become a Soviet citizen was also deported. A part of the Sovietization process was to rid the area of bourgeois influence, and that included successful entrepreneurs. Being banished to Siberia in February was indeed a hardship on whole families. They were sent to the north near the arctic circle and east close to the Sea of Japan in the Soviet Union.

The second group was comprised of families of those who were previously arrested, such as families of soldiers who had recently fought in the September campaign defending Poland, and those who were known to have anti-Soviet views. This deportation took place on April 12 and 13, 1940, which accounted for over 320,000 people being displaced forcibly from their homes and into Kazakhstan.

The third group was rounded up in June/July 1940, which took 240,000 people from their homes.

The last major deportation occurred in June 1941, taking over 300,000 people and occurring just as the Germans were invading Soviet territory. Even as the Nazis invaded the Soviet Union, Stalin continued to victimize Polish citizens with forced deportation; these families were being transported in train cattle cars while the German Luftwaffe strafed the countryside above them. The total populace deported from all the roundups was between 1.2 to 1.7 million Polish citizens, whose only crime was being a Pole and living in the land the Russians lost during the Polish-Russian border war in 1920.[14]

My dad's family lived in a town called Styj in the Kresy region. There were four members in dad's family: his sister Stasia, short for Stanisława, his mother Paulina, and father Marian. Their day for deportation came in April 1940 when the Soviets were at their door. His sister had been living with her parents after her husband Adam Smarzewski, a reserve army Second Lieutenant, went off to war to defend Poland against the German invasion the September before. He was captured and arrested. Stasia married Adam in the spring of 1938 and in April 1940, she received a letter from her husband wishing her a happy anniversary. The very next day, she and her parents were deported. Stasia knew he had been captured after the Soviet invasion and was in a Soviet prison called Starobielsk, and also knew that he and the other prisoners were then taken somewhere north and vanished "like stones in the water," as she described it in one of her letters to my dad. The anniversary wish was the last time she ever heard from her husband.

The three of them were rounded up on that April day in 1940 because Stasia was the wife of an Army officer, and her parents had a son, my dad, who was also a reservist soldier who went off to defend Poland. Stasia knew her husband had been captured, yet at that time, no one knew what had happened to her brother. Dad's aunt, uncle, and cousin were also involved in this same roundup.

---

[14] The figures vary because no one source can agree with the other. Soviet record-keeping was not always reliable.

His cousin was married to a soldier who fought in the September campaign. Both families were taken to the steppes of Kazakhstan SSR. The word "steppe" describes the semi-arid grassland area which stretches for thousands of miles across Eurasia and has the most severe climate. The new slaves for Stalin were dispersed among the kolkhozes and sovkhozes, the cooperative and state-run farms, where all were forced to work. The roundup happened before dawn and this hit the town of Styj like a tremor. Many families were forced at gunpoint to abandon their homes and leave at all hours of the night.

It did not matter whether you were an infant, a pregnant woman, elderly, infirmed, or disabled. You were told to pack up what belongings you could carry in an hour, sometimes less, abandon your home, and be carted away in wagons and shipped off by trains to Siberia. This was deportation. You were taken from your own country and then dropped off to another. The final destination was somewhere in Siberia, which is a vast region of Russia including what is now northern Kazakhstan. The massive region called Siberia constituted all of northern Asia, which extends from the Ural Mountains in the west to the Pacific Ocean in the east and southward from the Arctic Ocean to the hills of north-central Kazakhstan, SSR and the borders of Mongolia and China. These families and other dissidents were taken by train to remote areas in cattle cars where the accommodations were not those of civilized society, with sixty to seventy frightened people in each car using a hole in the floor for the toilets. No food or water was given for days at a time.

Those chosen for deportation were deliberately chosen because of their relationship with someone in the military, past or present, successful entrepreneurs, and influential government officials on all levels. It was the Soviet's intent to break down any local structure or resistance, in addition to getting the needed slave labor in the Siberian regions. This effort was to help the Russian economy with their war machine and for the Sovietization of the occupied territory. Such deportation was the fate of my dad's family, his parents, and his sister.

How did the Soviets know whom to deport and for what reasons? After the Soviet invasion in mid-September 1939, the culture of day-to-day life in all the occupied villages changed. October brought "free" elections where new government officials needed to replace the influential Poles of pre-war society. The previous officials were now either dead or deported to Soviet Siberia. Communist sympathizers were put on the ballot to replace the Polish officials. Those who considered themselves sympathizers were mainly Jews and Ukrainians, and they welcomed the Russians into town. Because of the biases imposed by the Polish society of the past, this population had been locked out of government positions by the Second Republic's government. Those who were Ukrainian Nationalists, however, did not consider themselves Communist; as a result, they were equally repressed by the new regime just like ethnic Poles. Everyone in each town and village had to vote, even if sick or infirmed. Once the election took place, the sympathizers or those who had Communist ties were elected. They now helped the Soviets enforce the new order.

My mother, after her release from a gulag, was asked to share her thoughts about life in Kosów Huculski during those early months of Soviet occupation, describing how life had changed.[15]

She explained that the new order had the Jews and Ukrainians in leadership roles, ousting the native Poles. This was done by the main muscle in town, the NKVD. If a Pole was needed for an important function that no one else could perform, if he was still around, he was reinstated but at a lower rank. If he objected to this mistreatment, he was arrested and shipped off to Siberia. The new order started with the arrests of shop owners who owned businesses, such as grocers, shoe store owners, and fabric store owners, "the bourgeoisie wealthy" as they were called by the Soviets. Random people would also be called in for questioning. "Those souls never returned," she said. The ruble replaced the zloty, the Polish currency, and the price of produce and goods went up 200%, which created poverty. Shop owners had their property

---

[15] My mom's statement - Hoover Institution Archives

simply taken from them in broad daylight. People in Styj were thrown out of their homes so Red Army officers could live there, while schools were closed to house the Red Army soldiers.

Before the elections, the Soviets held "party meetings" which everyone was told to attend. There was so much fear among the people that everyone did attend. A commandant was assigned to every ten homes to hold block meetings. These political meetings were organized to intimidate and instill fear while teaching, or better said brainwashing, the Communist Party line. It was the Poles, who were the wealthy bourgeoisie, who needed to be re-educated. At these meetings, the commandant was able to learn all about his assigned families and knew which families had an officer or soldier who fought in the September Campaign or was captured and imprisoned.

Because each commandant knew where "his" families lived, if someone was ill, he paid them a visit to their home so they could cast their ballot.

When it came time to prepare the lists of who would be deported, or who would receive a favorable report and therefore not be deported, the local Communist sympathizers, which included some Jews and Ukrainian Communists, helped decide the fate of many Poles. The nighttime home invasions and subsequent deportations were based on adequate documentation of who should leave and why, targeting political and class enemies, and in some cases, allowing for the settlement of old scores between people.

When the banging on the door arrived for my dad's family the Serbiński's on April 12, 1940, they had a short time to pack up a few of their necessities and valuables before abandoning their home. There were rumors all over town about a potential roundup and many families had prepared by hiding valuables within garments, even sewing valuable silver or money or other items into skirt hems and other disguises so they could take those items with them for future security, such as bartering for food.

Names of the targeted were on a list and they were given orders to take household items and clothing up to 100 kg in total weight, or 220 lb. During this frightening process, if someone protested or tried to resist, they were in danger of being harmed by the butt of a rifle or even being shot. While conducting the evacuations, the Russians would pull out drawers and dump their contents into the center of rooms and they would help themselves to what they wanted and leave the rest in a heap. They were looking for hidden weapons. This was done at my dad's house and once his family left their home, a friend came in the morning and took from the piles of belongings strewn all over the house a few documents, like dad's birth certificate and photos that the friend knew should be saved.

Dad's family was sent to Kojbagor, Kustanajska Oblast. Oblast is an administrative district or region in Kazakhstan SSR of the Soviet Union. In some instances, hundreds of people were simply dropped off in the middle of the Steppes of Kazakhstan, with nothing around them for miles. They had to try to survive by building mud huts for shelter. Others were taken further into Siberia and whether a child, a pregnant woman, or an elderly person, one had to endure harsh and dangerous conditions. Their unbelievable circumstances included eating dead animals, even rats, just to survive. In the early weeks, many died simply because they did not have the will to live. The frail, elderly, and young children were the most vulnerable to the conditions and became immediate casualties.

Chapter 18

Zdzisław, My Dad

Dad's parents were deported in the spring of 1940 because their son fought in the September Campaign of 1939. It was now seven months later; so, where was he during the first months of the war?

The story I heard growing up was that he fought in the Polish Army, fled to Lithuania where he was interned as a POW, and then escaped. How did that happen? How did he escape? What happened after he escaped, and where did he go? I had many questions but as a child, I asked no further questions and let my imagination create the rest of the story. My dad had been gone for thirty-eight years and I regret never asking my mom those questions when she was healthy enough to give me answers. I don't have much information about my dad's September Campaign experience. Everything I have found out is from piecing together facts from his military service records after requesting and receiving information from Polish military archives and doing research in the context of what I remember from my childhood. My dad was close-mouthed about his military experience, particularly with his children. I am so grateful my mother shared more when she did. Too many times, the important stories which should be told are silenced by such comments as "No one wants to talk or hear about those days," and then the answers go to the grave with the war veteran. The saved documents from that era, the correspondence from family members which mom saved, help to draw a timeline of where he was and why. Many details previously unknown to me came from the Polish military archives in London, along with my dad's military documents that mom saved. This helped me to fill in some of the gaps for those years.

The first letter my dad's family received from him during the war was dated July 7, 1942, nearly a year after Stalin granted amnesty to imprisoned Poles. My dad was in Kermine, Uzbekistan, while the family wrote from Kojbagor, Kazakhstan.

So how did my dad get to Kermine? It was already 1942 and the war started in 1939. Knowing that my dad was assigned to the 29th light artillery regiment of the 29th Infantry does make it easier to conclude that he was out of the Grodno Garrison and mobilized to defend the city of Wilno against the invading German and Soviet Red Army. This area is in the Northeastern part of the old Poland, now Lithuania. The Battle of Wilno occurred toward the end of September when the city was scarcely fortified. Most of the military might and resources had already been scattered throughout Poland earlier in the month in an effort to defend the country against the Germans. Civilian volunteers fought alongside the soldiers and it was clear that the unarmed civilians needed to retreat to sympathetic Lithuania for safety while the armed militia and army kept fighting. Armaments were scarce and with scouting reports confirming large numbers of advancing Soviet troops from the east. This caused the commanding general to order all units to fall back toward the Lithuanian border.

The Soviets were able to secure the city on September 19, 1940, and all Polish soldiers either surrendered or withdrew to Lithuania. I had always heard the story that my dad retreated to Lithuania as did nearly 15,000 Polish soldiers and civilians, where they were interned by the Lithuanian Government.

According to the Lithuanian Red Cross, 14,000 Polish soldiers were granted non-hostile internment in Lithuania. As of September 23, 1940, my dad was in a Lithuanian POW camp, possibly Alytus-Olita, but I don't know for sure. This camp, which was created in a deserted resort, was set up for Polish soldiers. This camp and the town of Alytus were close to the Polish border and both are relatively close to Wilno, which makes sense. The Lithuanian government was neutral and welcomed retreating Polish soldiers and set them up in transitory camps which were not hostile, and many POWs who escaped from these internment/POW camps did so without much resistance from camp officials. The Lithuanian officials looked the other way from escaping Polish soldiers because the government needed to reduce the size of the camp populations to lower expenses incurred to house and feed the foreign soldiers and civilian refugees. Since I know he escaped from an internment camp in Lithuania which was likely the one in Alytus from his military records, I learned that dad went to Panevėžys, Lithuania, a town further north of the camp, in the middle of January 1940. Many friendly Lithuanians who lived there were willing to hide and help Polish soldiers as long as they could. Upon escape, my dad found work in a sugar factory where he did some maintenance work as a welder and also helped run the steam furnace. He did this for well over a year until Poles, as well as native Lithuanians and Jews, were no longer safe in the region, as the country was being taken over by the Soviets. By the end of April 1941, my dad was arrested by the Soviets and sent off to a facility that housed political prisoners in Gorky, Russia, north of Moscow, today called Novgorod, Russia, just south of the former Leningrad, today St. Petersburg.

Prior to September 1941, over 20,000 Polish POWs and hundreds of thousands of civilians remained in Soviet captivity until their release following the signing of the Sikorski-Majski agreement, allowing for amnesty. In my dad's case, for whatever reason, he was not released until the end of December 1941, and documents reveal it took him only nine days to travel to Bukhara, Uzbekistan, one of the Polish Army collection sites.

Chances are he was able to take a train to Bukhara and did not have to walk. They welcomed former POWs back into the new Polish Army. The Second Corps was led by General Władysław Anders, also a former Soviet prisoner himself. This Army created on Soviet soil became known as "Ander's Army." Not knowing how dad got to one of the collection sites, he was able to join the wartime Polish Army on January 7, 1942, ready to begin his light artillery training in Kermine and hoping one day to fight the Germans.

Chapter 19

Katyń

Kozielsk, Starobielsk, Ostarsków—these are the names of special prisons located in Russian towns. They housed prisoners considered most dangerous (Polish Army officers, soldiers assigned to border protection, policemen; reservists who were doctors, lawyers, university professors, landowners, as well as priests and other influential citizens from towns all over the Kresy Region). Most of the resident prisoners were captured and imprisoned in the early weeks of the Soviet invasion and during the early months of the occupation.

In March 1940, Stalin made the decision to exterminate Polish prisoners of war who were detained in those three camps as well as additional prisoners from western Belarus and Ukraine. The order was signed by six members of the Soviet Politburo and Stalin himself who authorized the execution of 25,000 Polish as "nationalists and counterrevolutionaries" in order to deprive Poland of future Polish military and political leadership. This group of prisoners, the well-trained officers, also included influential members of government, successful businessmen, clergy, university professors, doctors, lawyers, judges, musicians, writers, and poets.

Eliminating this group of people would eliminate the possible influence they would have on Polish culture if they returned. Since Stalin was not a party to the Geneva Convention on the treatment of prisoners and rules of war, it was easier for him to murder over 25,000 people between April and May 1940. The collective tragedy is referred to as the Katyń Massacre.

This war crime was committed by NKVD, the secret police, authorized by Joseph Stalin.

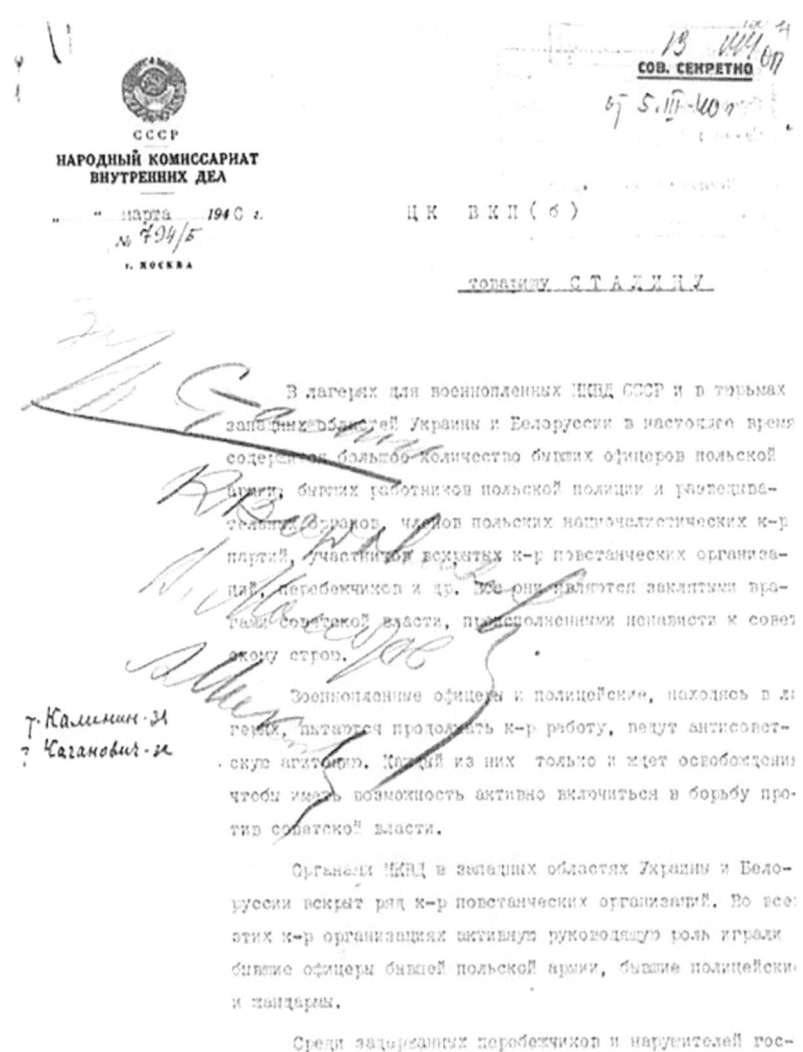

This document, dated 1940 was released in 1990 bearing responsibility for the murders. Stalin's signature is the first one, the one at the top.

Once captured, the officers were separated from the enlisted lower ranks, many of whom were delivered to the Germans or were sent back to their towns in Poland. In addition to the career officers and reservist officers, others in Polish society were targeted with arrest having their names on the execution list. To prevent civilized Polish society from having an anchor of organized retaliation, intellectuals and influential people were affected. Those who were besieged and found themselves in the three death camps came from various other transitory camps from Ukraine and Russia over the course of five to six months.

Conditions in the camps varied as the numbers increased. Some blocks had better food and more food than others, while sleeping arrangements were dismal, dirty, and insect-ridden. During the six months of incarceration, the prisoners were interrogated not just about military matters but about political leanings, such as being anti-communist. After all, each of the prisoners was an offender, a member of a "bourgeois army" and participated in a "world counter-revolution" against the Soviet Union. Following these interrogations and cross-examinations, some inmates started to disappear from camp. In December, 1939, around Christmas, there was only one chaplain left in camp. In the early part of March 1940, some others left camp and the story was that they were removed and sent to various other prisons for further interrogation. Some were sentenced to detention in labor camps. Those who disappeared undoubtedly were killed.

Rumors began to circulate in the Kozielsk camp that it would be liquidated. It was hinted that the prisoner population was to be redistributed among other camps since Kozielsk was overcrowded. In April, the evacuation of the prisoners began. A survivor recounts his day-to-day experience in Kozielsk, and how thousands of prisoners left systematically while the rest, still being held, had no idea where the others were going. Those left behind each time were envious of those leaving, as they all were convinced they were being released to go home. Then, Soviet authorities officially announced that the officers were going home. Those prisoners who were from Eastern Poland under the Soviet occupation were to return to their villages. Those from the Western areas would be handed over to the Germans. With this information, the prisoners of Kozielsk were elated. They were going home.

Some of the first to leave were three generals. As a gesture of goodwill, the Soviet commander gave them a going-away luncheon, which was followed by wildly cheering prisoners as they left. The mood was so upbeat on that beautiful sunny day with the fellow officers saluting and cheering their generals! Almost every day thereafter, groups of at least 200 officers were taken away. There was no logic to which ranking officer was selected to go in any one group, which for those who remained was very confusing. The population of the camp got significantly smaller. Those left behind were starting to feel depressed because they were not on the list to go home. The Poles were encouraged to believe they would be released, but the NKVD interviews were, in effect, a selection process to determine who would live and who would die. One Soviet Guard whispered to one of the prisoners, "Don't grumble. The later you go, the better for you." This systematic genocide continued at the other camps during the same period.

The camp evacuations continued through May 1940. By mid-month, there was a list of prisoners who were to stay; the others were to leave. Those leaving were sent in trains then trucks under deplorable conditions. Those transported received no water, were tightly crammed in the trucks, and settled in Griazovec, which had been a monastery prison not too far from Moscow. On their journey, the prisoners from Kozielsk met up with a previous group that had been evacuated on a date in late April. But where were the hundreds or thousands of others? When the prisoners asked the Soviet guards when they were going home like the others, the reply was, "When have you ever heard of prisoners of war being released before the war is over?" The guards' innuendoes suggested that the others perished under the hoax of being released.

The place most identified with this murderous massacre is the Katyń Forest, which is twelve miles west of Smolensk, Russia. The victims were walked into the woods, had their hands tied behind their backs, then were shot in the backs of their heads execution-style. They were bayoneted and buried in huge but shallow mass graves which held multiple layers of bodies. At other sites, these murders occurred in prison basements, or NKVD headquarters basement in Smolensk, with the bodies then taken away by truck and buried in nearby mass graves. Many of these victims were not only career officers and policemen but military reservists. This huge number of executions included a number believed to be over 14,000 career Polish Army officers. One executioner, Vassily Milkhailovich Blokhin, claimed that he killed 6,000 men in twenty-eight days. Those killed at Katyń included 1 admiral, 2 generals, 24 colonels, 79 lieutenant colonels, 258 majors, 654 captains, 117 naval captains, 3,420 non-commissioned officers (NCOs), 7 chaplains, 3 landowners, 1 prince, 43 officials, 85 privates, and 131 refugees. Also, among the dead were 2 university professors, 300 physicians, several hundred lawyers, engineers, and teachers; more than 100 writers and journalists as well as about 200 pilots.[16] Many of the victims were reservists who had been mobilized when Germany invaded. One such reservist was my dad's brother-in-law, his sister's husband, Adam Smarzewski. He was my uncle, but the truth of the matter is that I don't know anything about him other than his name. There was no conversation in my house growing up about this tragedy. I was told that the Soviets killed Adam and that was it. Nevertheless, since learning the gravity of this massacre, and based on my Polish pride, I do feel personally violated knowing that he was a victim of this genocide. In all, the NKVD eliminated almost half the Polish officer corps, which was part of Stalin's long-range effort to prevent the resurgence of an independent Poland.

Interestingly, one of the first graves was unearthed by the German Army while advancing into Soviet territory three years after the massacre. Stalin of course accused the Nazis of this

---

[16] The Katyń Controversy: Stalin's Killing Field — Central... - CIA.gov, by Benjamin B. Fischer.
https://www.cia.gov/library/center-for-the-study-of-intelligence/csi.../art6.html
Apr 14, 2007.

brutality. The Polish government, upon learning of this horrific crime, insisted on independent forensic experts to evaluate the situation, and those experts confirmed that indeed, it was the Red Army that was responsible for the murder of nearly 25,000 Polish officers and high-profile civilians. Some even estimate that the figure could be as high as 27,000. As a result of this accusation, Stalin broke off all diplomatic ties with the Polish government in London and closed the borders to any additional Poles leaving the Soviet Union. History has confirmed that the Kremlin covered up the facts and the allies, who needed Stalin's support during the rest of the war, allowed the cover-up to go on.

At the post-war Nuremberg Trials, the Katyń matter was on the agenda but then removed due to Stalin's influence. It was not until the Iron Curtain fell in 1990, 44 years later, that the Kremlin declassified some documents about the executions and issued an apology to the Polish government for this heinous war crime. Bodies were exhumed and identified from seven mass grave sites. Many items that were excavated proved these soldiers were Polish officers. These items were recovered and preserved. Since the soldiers thought they were "going home," they had all of their possessions with them, including razors, matches, cups, eating utensils, rosaries, combs, scissors, and coins. There were buttons, epaulets from uniforms, wedding bands, dog-tags, glasses, coats, even grain in a leather pouch. That soldier thought he might get hungry during the transport "home."

Excavated items from common graves.

Adam, my dad's brother-in-law, was imprisoned in Starobielsk, one of the three prisons involved in the Katyń Massacre. The last communication from him was April 1940, right before dad's sister and his parents were deported and exiled to Siberia, as were thousands of families of those soldiers executed in Katyń.

It was not until September 2012 that final documents were declassified from Russian central archives relating to the massacre. Nothing new was revealed except information confirming that President Roosevelt was fully aware of the massacre. He suppressed the information so as not to offend Stalin with an accusation of a war crime. President Roosevelt believed that Stalin was a good leader and felt he could be controlled politically, but Roosevelt primarily needed "Uncle Joe," which was the benevolent term for this tyrannical despot, and also the Red Army to defeat Hitler and then help the United States to fight Japan. However, there was no political control of Stalin as we all know now. Stalin had his own plan, which included the total domination of Eastern and Central Europe.

Today, there is a museum in Warsaw dedicated to preserving the memory of the Katyń Massacre, where recovered and preserved items are on display. I have been there twice, bringing my daughter with me the second time. I find the place fascinatingly eerie because the museum itself feels like a burial ground. The reality is that what has been recovered and preserved once belonged to real people. The Katyń Massacre is more than a sad story.

Chapter 20

Anders' Army

Polish Lt. General Władysław Anders was a career soldier who commanded a cavalry brigade during the September Defensive Campaign in 1939. He was wounded numerous times, captured, jailed, and tortured by the Red Army in the famous Lubyanka prison in Moscow. He was born in 1892 in the Kingdom of Poland, a part of the Russian Empire at the time when the country was still partitioned. He was the son of a Prussian father and Polish mother, educated at the Riga Polytechnic and, as a young officer, he served Tsar Nicholas II in the 1st Krechowiecki Lancers' Regiment during World War I. In the 1920s, he joined the Army for the Polish Second Republic and rose to the rank of general by the mid-1930s. Don't be fooled by the German last name and the fact that he was raised a Protestant as almost all Poles are Roman Catholic. He was one with the Polish people and with the land he fought for and loved. Eventually, he converted to Catholicism.

As a result of the Polish-Soviet (amnesty) agreement of July 1941, a new army was to be formed on Russian soil. General Anders, who was also freed from prison in Moscow, was named commanding general of this new army. The Poles who had been deported and soldiers who were imprisoned were set free from all parts of the Soviet Union, all trying to make their way to Uzbekistan to find freedom from brutality, starvation, and diseases. They hoped to eventually fight the Germans and to find hope for a future. Men, as well as women and children, made their way to the safe haven of the new Polish Army collection areas, hoping to be conscripted or serve in some way in order to receive food and clothing, just as my mom did. Anders found these people half-starved and in rags. Out of the 1.7 million people deported from their homes in Eastern Poland, only a few hundred thousand made it out of Siberia alive. These women, children, and elderly followed the army as their only means of survival since the Soviets refused to help the civilian refugees. Many children were orphaned as a result of the hardships of travel, lack of food, and diseases, primarily typhus. General Anders insisted that the travelers receive some of the rations provided to his soldiers. He constantly fought for more rations for his army, fighting for the well-being of the returning POWs, the starving men coming out of prisons and gulags, as well as the women and children who were leaving the horrors of their Siberian Gehenna.[17] General Anders was responsible for setting up orphanages for the thousands of children who lost their parents along the way in and out of the Soviet Union to starvation or disease. He also organized a Women's Auxiliary Service to be a service arm of the army. The auxiliary was known and referred to as PSK or Pomocnicza Służba Kobiet.[18] The auxiliary was designed to not only provide support services for the army, but to house, clothe, and feed the huge number of women and children coming his way from prisons and labor camps from all over the Soviet Union. "Anders' Army," as it was known, became the Polish Second Corps.

Anders and General Sikorski, a leader of the government in exile, met constantly with Soviet authorities as well as with Stalin to ensure that all Poles were released from incarceration. General Anders was dumbfounded by the low number of returning officers from POW camps to the collection areas. Certainly, there should be over 14,000 additional career officers and other reservists coming

---

[17] In Judaism, **Gehenna** (or Ge-hinnom) is a fiery place where the wicked are punished after they die or on Judgment Day, a figurative equivalent for "Hell" or Hades.

[18] PSK or *Pomoczniczna Wojskowa Sluzba Kobiet*, PSK is pronounced pestki in Polish. The word literally means seeds or stones of a fruit).

out of incarceration. It was as if they disappeared without a trace. Stalin feigned ignorance when asked why thousands of Polish officers had not made it out of POW camps. His only response was that he did not know what became of them, so they must have escaped to Mongolia. For many reasons, far more deportees remained in the Soviet Union than managed to leave. Many were sick or chose not to travel. They were lost or had travel papers stolen. Many were stranded.[19]

Other former soldiers and civilians, in their efforts to get to the collection areas, were delayed or detained by the Russian NKVD on technicalities such as not being issued proper travel papers or because their trains were diverted to other parts of the Soviet Union without their knowledge. One survivor story I came across was of a train stopping near a town and the conductor said that the train had broken down and he did not know when they would be able to leave again. The people onboard were starving and many left to walk to the nearby town looking for food. A young girl remembers her mother leaving to search for food for her and her two siblings. As you may well predict, the survivor went on to say that the train miraculously started working again, leaving those who went searching for food were left behind. The young girl never saw her mother again and she was left to care for her two younger brothers who shortly thereafter got sick and both died. She was ultimately sent to a Russian orphanage.[20] Such a method was the Soviet way of limiting the number of people leaving the country alive and going on to freedom. For whatever reasons, refugees would be stranded in the steppes of Kazakhstan. Having no supplies or rations, they either starved to death or were forced to work again at local state-run farms as Soviet citizens, or were conscripted into the Red Army.

Those who did make it to the safety of the Anders' Army did have many needs. On several occasions, General Anders tried

---

[19] Fewer than expected released from the Soviet Union by Stalin. *Trail of Hope*, by Norman Davis, pages 183-84.

[20] Testimony of child separated from mother looking for food. *Forgotten Odyssey,* a documentary film by Jagna Wright and Aneta Naszynska, 1999.

to obtain increased rations for his soldiers as well as to secure additional training supplies, such as warm clothing and actual training munitions. Training soldiers requires that they be healthy, fed, and possess the necessary equipment. General Anders was concerned that Stalin needed his men. If they were ill-prepared, Anders' men would be placed in a third-rate Russian Division and sent to their slaughter, or they would be separated and distributed among larger Russian units not lead by Polish officers.[21]

---

[21] Ill-prepared Polish soldiers possibly going to slaughter. *Trail of Hope*, by Norman Davis, page 125.

Chapter 21

Reaching Freedom

After weeks of walking, catching rides on mule carts, and the occasional train ride, my mother and her traveling companions reached Bukhara in the Soviet state of Uzbekistan where there was a Polish delegation speaking their native language. They were delighted to hear Polish spoken everywhere and relieved that they had made it. Arriving there and learning that civilians could be conscripted into the Polish Army and put to work to help the war effort against Nazi Germany was a gift for so many women and children arriving daily. They would be able to regain their health by receiving regular meals, shelter, and clean clothes. Released Polish people who made it to an area where there was a Polish delegation were able to receive aid in the form of food, clothes, and money.

After answering many questions, documenting where they had been and what they experienced, my mother and her travel companions were registered, fed, and given train tickets to travel to the women's center which was set up in a nearby town. They were told they would be given jobs to do based on their interests and skills to support the army. Such jobs were either in the motor pool, where they could learn how to repair and drive vehicles and heavy equipment, provide office support for all the paperwork, be trained in the nursing corps, help with the cooking, or become teachers for the hundreds of arriving children. The organization that General Anders created for women was known as the Polish Women's Auxiliary Army Services or PSK.

Theoretically, the idea of arriving into the safe hands of their countrymen, where they would receive food and shelter, was a perfect objective for them and for all who had suffered so much over the last two years. The reality was that my mother and her companions arrived in a Polish safe haven but they also arrived in a typhus epidemic. There were sick people everywhere. So many were seriously ill that when they tried to get to the local medical facility that had been set up, countless people did not make it. There were dead bodies collecting in streets and in ditches all around the town. Typhus had claimed many of those who fought hard and long to escape enslavement and gain their freedom. It was nothing unusual to see mule-drawn carts with corpses piled high. These poor souls would be buried in common graves.

Not long after my mother arrived in Bukhara, she contracted typhus. The disease is quite common in unsanitary and overcrowded conditions. Typhus is not to be confused with typhoid fever, as they are each distinct and caused by different species of bacteria. Typhus was common in prisons where carriers, usually lice or rats, spread the disease.[22]

The first course of action in treatment was to shave the head of the infected patient to rid the body of lice. Outbreaks tend to be more prevalent in the winter months when blankets are shared and more clothing is worn. A typical typhus outbreak, such as this one occurring in the winter, suggests that my mother got to Uzbekistan sometime in the winter of 1941–42, after her release from the gulag the previous fall. Sanitation was still an issue. Even though the terms "medical facility" or "hospital" suggest

---

[22] Typhus: The disease spreads easily especially when prisoners huddled together in dark, filthy conditions. Typical symptoms of this disease are high fever—up to 104° F, delirium, low blood pressure, back pain, photophobia (sensitivity to light), severe headaches, and muscle pain. Without treatment, death may occur in ten to sixty percent of patients with epidemic typhus, with patients over age sixty having the highest risk of death. http://www.medicinenet.com/typhus/ page2.htm.

sanitary conditions, the conditions were anything but sanitary. Gravely ill people were warehoused in a building, lying on the floor, with nurses stepping over other patients to care for those who needed the most care, administering what few medical supplies they had. My mother said this went on for months. She recalls her head being shaven as per protocol and that she fought the disease with everything she had. When her fever broke, she was a shadow of her former self and it took her weeks to regain enough strength to even walk across the room without falling down.

Meanwhile, back in camp, everyone was talking about a potential transport to the Middle East where the Polish Army would begin training. The idea of leaving the brutality and oppression of the Soviet Union behind set a hopeful tone throughout the camp.

The thought occurred to me that it is possible that both my mom and dad were at this camp at the same time but did not encounter each other. I don't have exact dates for either of their arrivals, but I do know that they both went to Bukhara to register for Anders' Army.

Chapter 22

Anemones at the End of Their Journey

In order to train an army, the soldiers needed to be recovered from illness, be well-fed, well-clothed, and well-equipped. Because so many civilians needed care, food, and shelter, General Anders was sharing his soldiers' rations with the civilian population. He was always pleading with Stalin for increased rations. At the same time, he would ask Stalin to have his men moved further south to a warmer climate which would help them regain their health. The ultimate goal was to move out of the Soviet Union to be closer to the British Army which was centralized in Iran.

Supporting the Polish Army and their civilians was becoming a financial liability to Stalin, even though he provided rations for 26,000 soldiers. The problem was there were 115,000 military and civilian mouths to feed, so those 26,000 rations were hardly enough. After much political posturing and negotiating, Stalin, seeing this as a liability, permitted the Poles to leave the Soviet Union for Iran to be a part of the Allied military effort, and to have the British take over the care of the Polish problem.

Because Stalin granted the amnesty, he wanted the Polish army to be fighting on his behalf on the Soviet-German front in the fall of 1941, even though Anders' men were emaciated, in rags, starving, and untrained. That goal was unrealistic. They would have been slaughtered. Therefore, Anders did everything he could to resist this threat and pressed to have them moved.

Letters from the Box in the Attic

At this time, my mother was recovering from typhus and was hoping to be trained in a special support function for the Polish Army as a nurse. Beginning in March 1942, military personnel and civilians began their crossing of the Caspian Sea from Krasnovodsk, Turkmenistan, SSR to the port of Pahlavi, Iran, known today as Bander-e Anzali. After the first wave of evacuations in March and April, additional military and civilian men, women, and children were transported in August to Pahlavi.

From across the Caspian Sea, the Iranian and British officials watched the first Soviet tanker cross the Sea, listing as it steamed into the harbor at Pahlavi. They had little idea of how many Polish refugees were on board. Only days before, they had expected only military personnel. These officials had no knowledge as to the physical state of all the evacuees and what to expect in general since only days earlier, they learned that civilian women and children were to be transported as well as military troops. This tanker would be one of the many grossly overcrowded ships making this run from late March to early April, then again, in August 1942. These passages proved to be treacherous as there was standing room only on board with little water to drink. People were getting sick everywhere, but nevertheless, they were ecstatic to be leaving that godforsaken country, the USSR.

Reading mom's accounting of this period reminds me of the Haitian Boat People of the late 20th century when so many Haitians tried to make their way to the United States looking for a better life. Many drowned and eventually, the rest were turned away. And what of the Syrian refugees, fleeing their horrors, only to have their boats capsize, resulting in bodies of men, women, and small children washing up on the shores of Greece? We will always have these mental images depicting human suffering of historical proportion. In my mother's experience, the passage was difficult but ultimately successful.

The two evacuations that year collectively brought 115,000 people to the other side of the Caspian Sea: 60,000 recruits, 37,000 civilian adults and 18,000 children out of the Soviet Union, only seven percent of the number originally exiled or imprisoned by the Soviets. [23] The number saved is low because so many died during the various legs of their journey, or were left behind in the Soviet Union. The Iranian Army provided 2000 tents, which stretched for several miles along the shoreline of the Caspian Sea. It was a vast complex of bathhouses, latrines, sleeping quarters, disinfection booths, laundries, and a hospital. Even with the extent of this makeshift city, it was still inadequate. With so many people in one area, diseases continued to decimate the population of the refugees.

My mother was one of the lucky ones to be on one of the first transports leaving Krasnovodsk to Pahlavi, along with many seriously ill men, women, and children. By that time, she was healthy enough to work and was sent on to Tehran to receive nurse's training while some of her traveling friends from Siberia took on some of the other jobs. It was critical to train as many women as possible in nursing because of the tremendous needs of sick civilians and the military. Mom's training was set up in a makeshift hospital at an old airport in Tehran.[23]

Nurses and doctors—mom is peeking over the soldier's shoulder.

---

[23] http://www.parstimes.com/history/polish_refugees/exodus_russia.html

She had to complete an eight-week practical nursing course through the Polish Red Cross and subsequently received additional certifications in emergency care. Emma was so proud to be a nurse, to be able to help people. She was grateful to be out of the captivity that had been strangling her for two years. She did say her time spent in Tehran was a positive and peaceful experience.

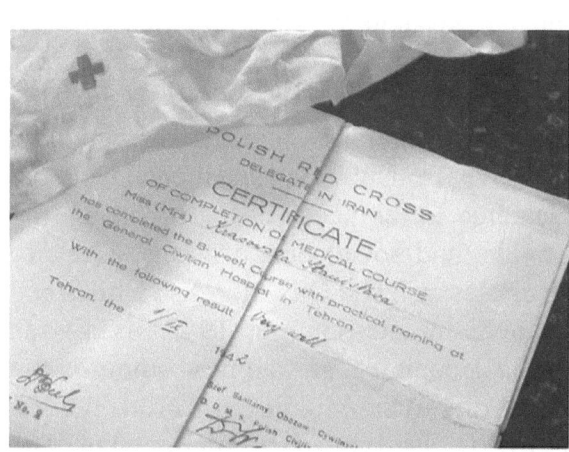

My mother became a nurse in the Polish Army on September 1, 1942

Mom on the right

Mom became a junior nurse in the Polish Army on 9/1/1942.

The nurses and doctors busily prepared for the ill and malnourished civilians and soldiers who needed care. By April 1, 1942, she, her companions, and many newly conscripted civilians and returning soldiers were now in the Polish Second Corps and officially under the command of the British Army. She had survived her odyssey from Eastern Poland, to Western Russia, to Asia, to the Middle East (crossing three continents).

Various diseases came to Tehran from the tented city on the shores of Pahlavi. Nurses had to deal with malaria, gastrointestinal amebiasis, dysentery, night blindness, scurvy, and typhus. My mother remembered suffering was everywhere, but nobody complained. They were grateful to be out of the Soviet Union and out of Stalin's clutches. Nevertheless, Poles were still dying everywhere. 2,000 Poles were buried in cemeteries all around Tehran and Pahlavi. Many thousands of the ill were children, either orphaned or separated from family by the harsh passage out of Soviet Russia. They were painfully emaciated and malnourished. Orphanages were immediately set up in Pahlavi, Tehran, and Ahvaz to care for these little souls on a transitory basis.

The first major orphanage was in Mashhad, run by Christian nuns. Eventually, it was Isfahan that became the major care center for Polish orphans, especially those under the age of seven. This was a beautiful and serene city in Iran where the surroundings helped the little children recover from physical and mental wounds. Many areas of the city catered to the needs of the orphanage by setting up schools, hospitals, and social organizations. The city became known in Polish circles as "The City of Polish Children."

Once training was over in late summer 1942, mom was assigned to the Third Field Hospital that was near some of the training units of the Polish Army in the Middle East. From Tehran, she was transferred to Qisil-Ribat, Iraq, north of Baghdad. The field hospital was in the middle of the Iraqi desert. Soldiers set up large tents for the wards and the hospital needed to be functioning as soon as possible to serve the different army units that were to train in the desert. But many of the soldiers contracted diseases while in the Soviet Union or while crossing the Caspian Sea.

The hospital was ready within a month and the patients started rolling in. It did not take long for all their beds to be filled, mom remembered. She was assigned to the surgical ward, which became her specialty. One building stood out among the tents: it was the building that housed the operating rooms and the chief of surgery, Lt. Dr. Arthur Wrobels, who was a strict disciplinarian. He tolerated nothing that would jeopardize the health of the soldiers, even some minor dust. He would require all medical personnel to conduct the "white glove test." Yet after one's duties were done, as my mom put it, "He was the kindest man, someone you could go to and cry on his shoulder." He was a close friend and would always have useful advice.

This doctor's kindness reminded her of her father. Immediately, her thoughts went to wondering about her father as well as how her mother was doing back home without them. The last letter Emma received from her mother was while she was in the Kharkov prison.

In that last letter, mom learned that her mother had received a letter from Zdzich, the boy mom had met in Kosów before the war. He had asked about her, wondering where she was and what had happened to her. He too was a POW in Lithuania and learned that mom had been arrested and was in prison. So much had changed in a short period of time. It had only been a year since her imprisonment and release. Where was Zdzich? Was he freed as well following amnesty? Did mom even know he had been in a Soviet prison as well? There were too many questions and not enough ways to find the answers.

The Iraqi desert terrain was flat and there was sand as far as the eye could see. Mom said the sand "swallowed the sun in the evening and spit it out the next morning." The heat was intense with temperatures climbing from 100° to 140° F from 1:00 to 4:00 p.m. when nothing and nobody moved. However, if something did need to be done, or if the patients needed attention, it fell to the nurses to do it. Mom and her fellow nurses would wet down their uniforms every hour to cool off and do what was necessary for the patients. At night, everyone had a bucket of water near their beds to wet down the sheets in order to stay cool.

Reading her accounting of the intense heat in Iraq reminds me of when my son Christopher served in the Marine Corps. His first post boot camp deployment was the first of three tours of duty in Iraq following the start of the Iraqi War in 2003. That first tour was in the middle of summer 2003, and he described the heat this way: "Imagine using a hairdryer on the 'high' setting and blowing the heat directly on your face." That image has stayed with me anytime I think of describing intense heat. My mother was thrilled to let him know that she was stationed in Iraq near Baghdad and knew all about the heat.

Mom was in Iraq from November 1942 to July 1943, so part of this desert experience occurred in the wintertime. During the winter months, violent winds and monsoon rains are typical weather in that part of the world. She recounted hearing a story which the Arabs told, "that if a man kills his wife during monsoon season, he isn't punished for it; he apparently couldn't help himself."

The rain and the winds caused damage to the hospital, and each time, the damage was repaired or cleaned up; but what she remembers best is the desert metamorphosis that goes through as a result. Instead of sand, as far as the eye can see, there were red flowers called "anemones." This event was analogous to how she and her young friends felt. Each of them had experienced violent sandstorms caused by driven winds and torrential monsoon rains, representing their travels into and out of Soviet Russia. What emerged was hope for the future. They believed there would be anemones at the end of their journey. This optimism typifies how Emma viewed her world.

> (AUTHOR'S NOTE: Much of the detail of my mom's story comes from her written notes and letters. Fortunately, I had been in possession of this story since the late 1980s and then found the raw entries for it in her journal. My brother Andy and my mother traveled to the island of Kauai for a weeklong holiday.
>
> Visiting the Kauai Desert in Hawaii Volcanoes National Park brought back many memories which started flowing while she and Andy were waiting for their flight in the airport before their return trip. He encouraged her to document what she remembered. Her story actually began with the desert as a trigger, a déjà vu moment, while on Kauai.)[24]

---

[24] My mother's essay

2 Letters

Chapter 23

From Uzbek to the Middle East

My dad was not in the initial transport to Iran. Since his initial conscription was near Bukhara, Uzbekistan in January 1942, and because his background was light artillery, he was placed in the first artillery unit of the Polish Second Corps, training near Kermine. Conditions there, with the arrival of thousands of former soldiers, were dismal. Soldiers arrived starving, filthy, exhausted, lice-ridden, and in tattered clothes. Tents were set in the snow as housing but in those conditions, there was no warmth. Nonetheless, he was free!

My dad joined the 7th Light Artillery Regiment, later renamed the 7th Regiment of Horse Artillery. Before the war, he had trained with the 29th Light Artillery Regiment as an officer cadet, but now, his new unit was based in Kenimech, a small town in the Uzbek steppes near Kermine on the Tashkent railway line. There, he trained until the last evacuation of the Polish Second Corps soldiers in August.

The Soviets did not equip the fledgling Second Corps very well and the artillery supplied was no exception. But soon, they would be following orders and receiving supplies from the British Army. During the August evacuations, the last opportunity to leave Soviet soil, my dad sailed to Iran. It was during the summer of 1942, right before his passage, which he was able to finally locate and communicate with his family exiled in Kazakhstan. He had learned where they were living. While dad was still in

Uzbekistan, word got through to his family via another person, a good Samaritan, who delivered a postcard from my father in Uzbek to his parents telling them that dad was still alive. Just the thought of his parents receiving such a postcard is amazing. Letter writing was the sole means of communication; and if mailed, would the letter get to its intended receiver during the chaos of war? If a person was able to travel to another area, he or she was usually asked to deliver letters. There would be other good Samaritans in my family's lives.

That first correspondence between dad and his parents was in July 1942. They talked about dad being arrested and his time in a Soviet prison.

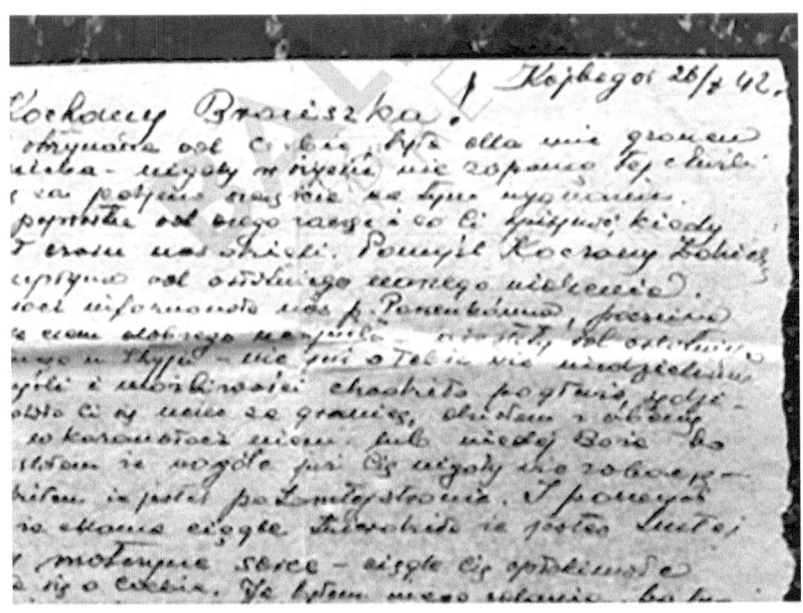

Dad joined the Polish Second Corp in 1942. Letter received from his exiled sister and parents living in Siberia.

His father replied to him, writing, "Zdzisek, my dear, write please and explain what you mean when you say that you probably won't be back to your previous condition. We don't understand what you wanted to tell us and we are wondering whether you, God forbid, are missing a body part." Since these letters, which my mom kept, are only one-way conversations between my dad and his parents, my dad must have answered that physically he was fine, but possibly, what he saw and/or experienced was not so fine and these experiences were life-changing. My grandfather went on to say that after much illness, they were all healthy now. However, he and dad's mom were worried about Stasia, dad's sister, because she had to work ten hours a day doing manual labor.

My grandfather also wrote about their living conditions: "Living conditions are deplorable as there are twenty-two people living in one barracks, living together and freezing in the winter." "Zdzisio (dad's name used as a term of endearment), dearest, don't worry about us. So far God has been helping somehow and we hope that our suffering will come to an end soon." His father also added, "Could you get a leave and come to visit us? Or perhaps, would it be possible to get us to where you are? I know there were some families that left for the Army training areas. Perhaps you could do something to get us near you?"

His mother wrote separately, "I have been praying to the Holy Mother of God since you left home (in 1939). My heart told me that you were somewhere here, not far from us. Only your poor dad and Stasia didn't believe it. They thought you were able to get out of Poland and to the west. I had a feeling you were in prison." She had dreamed about him and felt he was in harm's way. "Can you find out what happened to Adam (Stasia's husband)?"

Dad's sister Stasia was not home when the letter arrived as she worked so far away and was, therefore, rarely home. When she did receive the news that her brother was alive, she wrote back to her brother saying, "The news of you reached me like a bolt of lightning from the blue. I will never forget this moment and consider it as the only good thing here in this exile. Until this day, I feel like I am in a dream. I studied every letter of every word you wrote and still can't believe it. It is all a miracle." Those first letters from dad's family shared stories of the hardships my grandparents and aunt suffered while living in the steppes of Kazakhstan. When deported, they were shipped to a "kolhoz" or "sovkhoz," a Soviet collective or state-run farm with oppressive conditions, but since then, they were moved to a "novostrojka," a new building site, where Stasia worked to build a new rail line. She went on to tell her brother how their dad worked hard as a carpenter but was not paid well. Her work was back-breaking and exhausting as she worked with a shovel, digging dirt and carrying stones for a new bridge connecting railroad tracks. She did not know how long she could continue to do this. She was not strong enough and her health was poor. Construction on this railroad began in 1939 and lasted throughout the war.[25]

Stasia's letters to dad told of how she and her parents had been able to barter for food since they were exiled but now, the bartering had ended as their valuables were gone. They were not able to take too much with them in the first place when they were banished from their home and homeland and now, they had nothing left. Stasia also made a plea for my dad to rescue them from their suffering and find out about her husband Adam. She wrote, "Just think about it, you are the youngest and now you are our caretaker and our hope to get us out from this abyss. I grieve every day since we have not been unable to find Adam. Supposedly, those prisoners from Starobielsk were taken somewhere north - and they 'vanished like a stone in water.'"

This correspondence took place a year after formal amnesty was announced for the Polish people in the Soviet Union. So, why did dad's family not leave the steppes of Kazakhstan? Had they left, they quite possibly would be reunited with dad.

Stasia went on to say that they all wanted to leave in the fall of 1941, but she kept waiting for news about Adam, and then all four

---

[25] Two thousand people worked on this huge project and 730 of them were Polish deportees to Kazakhstan. All of them lived in earth-houses with no sanitation facilities. As high as 30% of the workers contracted malaria. Many of the Poles worked barefoot and half-dressed in the winter of 1943 because there was a shortage of clothes and shoes. http://ehistory.kz/en/contnents/view/1469, History of Akmolinski-Kartaly Railway construction (1939-1945).

of them would leave to go south to join the new Polish Army. They sold everything they could, preparing for the exodus, but terrible news from the recruitment centers about diseases and tremendous hardships traveled back to them, which deterred them from leaving. With no word from Adam and the last days of November upon them, they decided to stay the winter which turned out to be excruciatingly cold, but they survived. Stasia then also wrote, "Ask for a leave and if you are well enough, perhaps, you could visit us or you could manage to take us with you. Many civilians were accepted into the army, or perhaps with my specialty, I could find work and be a useful individual."

As these letters were exchanged, my dad was slated to be transported from Uzbekistan to the Middle East in August 1942. Stasia and dad's parents continued to plead for his help. Reading the letters and then having to answer them had to be emotionally difficult for dad to write. It pains me to think that now, after finally connecting with his family, there was nothing he could do for them. If only I had the letters from dad that wrote back.

During this period of time, my dad was also able to connect with and correspond with his aunt and cousin who had also been deported to Kazakhstan. Aunt Maria was his mother's sister and after amnesty, she and her adult daughter Jana tried to make their way out of the Soviet Union. Jana wrote a letter to dad, which was delivered by people traveling to Ermine from their location in Kazakhstan. She mentioned that she and her mother corresponded with dad's parents and sister up until amnesty the year before while they were still in Dustan, Kazakhstan. Letters would get lost or take forever to reach their destinations. People were like gypsies, moving from place to place; either following those joining the army or just trying to make it out of the Soviet Union however they could. People wrote many letters to their loved ones during the war, yet so few got through. Eventually, some did. I have a postcard sent to dad from his sister that has so many delivery stamps on it that it is a wonder that it did eventually reach him.

The other news of Cousin Janka was that her husband was captured by the Germans in September 1939, and the last she heard from him was from a prison in Hungary. At the time Janka was writing her letter to my dad, she mentioned to him, "Try to come quickly, as a lot of people come to visit their families since there is talk about civilians leaving for Africa. We long to see you after three years." She also asked, "Please, if you know of Pawel Kubis, let him know that his wife, Elzbieta and father are well." It's distressing to know how people hungered for information about loved ones, or struggled to stay in touch, while traveling from place to place just trying to survive.

Dad's aunt and cousin left Kazakhstan when amnesty was granted in August 1941, and by 1943, they were in Iran in a temporary civilian camp but not in Africa. Their journey had started on August 20, 1941, when they went south from Kustany, Kazakhstan to Dzumbul, which is on the border of Kyrgyzstan. Prior to their leaving, Aunt Maria (Ciocia Maria in Polish) wrote to dad's parents, thinking that they would be leaving as well. But her sister wrote back sounding desperate about their situation of selling all their belongings and not leaving. This was the last she heard from dad's parents. Since the Serbińskis decided not to go south that fall, remaining in exile, Ciocia Maria still looked for her sister at each stop in her journey, knowing better but hoping to find them along the way. Ciocia and Janka then made it to Tehran in the spring of 1942 with the civilians who left the Soviet Union, suffering great hardships. By January of 1943, Ciocia Maria became gravely ill with typhus and spent two months in the hospital in Tehran recovering while Janka, as Ciocia wrote, "Poor Janusia was left alone with strangers."

While her mother was in the hospital, Janka reached out to my dad again, having exchanged letters through the kindness of strangers. They asked about each other's families. Dad told her about his parents and sister staying in Kazakhstan and she about her father needing to stay behind as well. Their lives in Tehran were upside down and their fates uncertain. Dad mentioned that he could come to see her on a leave, as he was in Kirkuk, Iraq at the time, but she cautioned him that a visit probably would not work. It was rumored that civilian camp no. 2, the largest of five camps for civilians where she was living, would soon close. In the meantime, Janka walked daily many kilometers to the hospital to see her mother. She also wrote, "Take comfort, that there are new waves of Poles arriving from Soviet Russia to Iran every week." She signed the letter, "Think good thoughts."

Ciocia Maria recovered well and gave my dad some advice in a letter. "Be careful, please. Don't drink. Dear boy, you have to be healthy and well, and help and be a joy to your mother and sister to build Poland because there are not many of you beautiful boys left. Where is Adam? Is he alive? My God, my heart is breaking; so many young, healthy, noble-minded people... Where are they? We must trust in God." The letter was signed, "Sending you lots of kisses," with a note on the side, "We signed up to go to India."

Chapter 24

The Final Gift

In the winter, the anemones in the desert flourish, but soon after a rain, the hot temperatures return and the desert returns to its more normal appearance: sand, sand, and more sand. The patients flow through the hospital daily in Qisil-Rabit where mom is now stationed. They still need much care. The usual conversations ensue with new arrivals: "Have you seen so-and-so?" or "Do you know what happened to my brother, husband, friend, parent?" My mother's question was always the same: "Have you seen or know anything about Marcin Krasowski?"—her father.

There was one patient who suggests that my mother place an ad in the newly published Polish newspaper out of Bagdad, *Kurier Polski* (Polish Courier), to try and find her father, or at least to receive possible information about him. This patient is stationed in Baghdad and offers to place the ad for her when he returns to his unit. The newspaper gives soldiers and support personnel reports from around the world, including news about General Sikorski's travels to Washington, Mexico, and Scotland and some recently published prose and poetry. The newspaper is printed six times a week and has a classified section.

By placing an ad, at least my mother feels she is being proactive about finding the whereabouts of her father. But now, she had to wait for a response if there is to be one. In the meantime, she remembers the days growing up in Kosów and what a wonderful relationship she has with her father. She remembers how he would take her to his office which was near the salt mines where he worked on her days off school. The memories of their time together back home are constantly on her mind. She closes her eyes and could feel her father's warm, protective arms around her and she would feel safe and secure, just as she had as a little girl.

Time passed and there is still no word from the ad. She must find out about her father. There are rumors swirling around the hospital that the staff may pack up and move to Palestine, but no one knows anything for sure. She needs to hear something before they leave.

That time finally arrived, a response from the ad! She is ordered by her supervisor to report immediately to a certain tent on hospital grounds. What could it be about? Someone is there to see her? This must be serious. Her heart begins to pound. She is getting lightheaded. Who is it? Is it information about her father? What is the news? Is he alive? Is he dead?

As she enters the tent, she almost faints at the sight of the person standing before her. That moment, she says, is indescribable. Standing in front of her is a young man, a young handsome soldier, the young man from her past, someone she knows from before the war. O God, thank you! It is her old boyfriend, Zdzich, whom she dated while living in Kosów before the war, someone she cares deeply about. Thoughts of the past, the time they spent together in her hometown, played like a newsreel in her mind. The past seemed like light years ago. They had not seen each other since before the war started, four years ago.

She only knew that he was in the army and had written her mother and found out that mom had been arrested and was in a Russian prison, and mom knew that he (my father) was a POW in Lithuania. After three-plus years, to see each other again was stunning. She asked, "How did you find me?" He responded, "I read your ad."

At that moment, my mother remembered thinking, "This was the last gift my dad was able to give me. The first man in my life was able to give me the second man in my life." It was her dad's final gift to her.

Was everything right with the world now? I don't think either of them felt that way, after what each of them had experienced, and still, the war was raging. Life was anything but simple or "alright." However, since my dad re-entered my mother's life in February 1943, she said she started to believe that there may be a future for her after all. But that brief feeling of optimism as they caught up with each other's lives became overshadowed by sadness and grief. Many of the letters she wrote my dad after that initial meeting were dark and melancholic.

They were not stationed that far away from each other but still, they were not able to see each other often; therefore, there were many more letters. The initial exhilaration of finding a loved one from her past only revealed the reality that mom was probably alone in the world, without parents or extended family. Would she ever see any of them again? She suspected that her father was dead, even though she had received no such formal notice. She would write to my dad that life was not the same as when they dated before the war, and that they are not the same people they once were. These feelings revealed a depressed state of mind when she wrote to him, "Don't write and don't visit."

Thankfully, my dad was quite persistent. He was not that easily dissuaded. He kept up the communication hoping she would come around. There is a series of ten letters from dad to mom during that time pleading his case. She had numbered them and must have reread them dozens of times during her life.

My mother's state of mind gradually improved. That day in the tent when he had found her again he told her was an omen for the future. Their new reality was that they were meant to be together and she finally agreed. She began to believe that they should continue their relationship and possibly plan for a future. Her mental state did improve as she indicated in a letter later, admitting that she was beginning to feel like a love-struck, giddy school girl, waiting every day for a letter from him. Her heart would race; her cheeks would flush while opening a new letter from her Zdzich, her love. He was always on her mind, along with the idea that there was going to be a future. The thought that they might actually have a life together was something she had not been able to visualize or consider possible.

She asked in one letter if he remembered two important dates. Whether he did or not was immaterial, because she did. They first met in Kosów on February 9, 1939, and reunited in the Iraqi desert on February 9, 1943.

The summer of 1943 was a wonderful time in their lives, even though they were separated by the war—she in Qizil-Ribat at the field hospital and he training in Kirkuk with the 7th Light Artillery Regiment. That summer, after completing additional training, he was no longer a cadet officer; he was promoted to Second Lieutenant, and best of all, they were planning their wedding!

The idea of love lost and then found is one from fairy tales and movies. But this was a story of found love, a connection to pre-war innocence. Their story of dad answering the ad was one I heard many times growing up. Mom would reflect on the cursory details of her war experience when telling the story of running the ad and my dad answering it, but the details of her mental struggle about her life and trauma were found in those precious letters she saved. These are details she would never have shared with me. But I do know how valuable family was to her; and knowing that she felt so alone in the world had to play havoc with her emotional state, making her even more fragile. Due to dad's persistence, they were back together.

Chapter 25

New Lands, New Adventures

From Poland to Russia and Siberia, to Iran, then to Iraq, across the Black Desert of Jordan to Palestine and Syria followed by Gaza and Port Said, across the Suez Canal to Egypt then to Palagiano, Italy and up Italy's northern coast—this was not an exotic vacation but the places my parents experienced, good and bad, from 1939–1946.

Some of these areas were desert locations and how can a person resist an oasis when there was one nearby? Maybe my mother saw the old silent picture *The Sheik,* starring Rudolph Valentino, when she was growing up, or read books about the Arabian Nights which took place in the desert. While working in the field hospital, my mom decided to visit an oasis that was near her hospital. She wanted to see what an oasis and its people were like, and to satisfy her curiosity about them. Oasis was a place of respite and for gathering in an otherwise desolate environment. A person could replenish their water and procure supplies if on a journey. As it turned out, the one Emma visited was a meeting place for locals. "Arabs came there to exchange the news, gossip, smoke, drink, and talk," she said. "They sat mostly on the floor and had a good time and made lots of noise." There were restaurants and stores which were surrounded by dozens of lush palm trees, just like in the movies. This was a pleasant indicator that life could be normal during the war, people going about their daily lives. Many of the places they found themselves while training or on hospital duty may not have been exotic vacations, but were exotic in terms of being very different from where they had come from. Like the old *Wizard of Oz* reference, "Toto, I don't think we are in Kansas anymore;" theirs would be, "Zdzich, I don't think we are in Poland anymore!"

The wedding they were planning did happen. Stanisława and Zdzisław were married on October 3, 1943, in a Third Field Hospital tent in Palestine by a second lieutenant priest. Podpułkownik Dr. Stefan Lubkowski and Porucznik Ludwik Blondek were their witnesses. Mom mentioned to me that on her wedding day, the dress she wore was a nurse's uniform from which she had saved the belt as a memento. She kept this belt for over seventy-five years. I have it with all the other mementos of her past. She also received a white Polish prayer book from the priest who performed the ceremony. He signed, dated, and dedicated the book to mom as a gift. Shortly before I was married, mom gave me the prayer book. It is not only beautifully preserved but a valued keepsake. Having searched through all the papers, letters, and photos from the box, sadly, I found no photos of the wedding ceremony. There are some photos, presumably from their honeymoon, but they are only street-scene shots; none of them depicting the two of them enjoying the sights together.

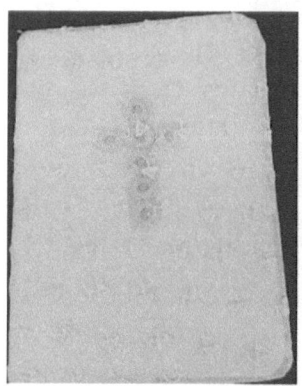

Prayer book and uniform belt and other memorabilia from mom's wedding day.

Staszka and Zdzich were able to honeymoon for two weeks traveling to Jerusalem and Bethlehem, visiting all the biblical sites of the Christian faith. She referenced her excitement upon visiting the Holy Land, because as a Catholic, as with those of the Jewish and Muslim faiths, these sites are historically sacred.

While I was growing up, my family had a beautiful Christmas nativity set with a straw-roofed barn. When decorating for Christmas, my brother and I would put cotton on the roof depicting snow as there needs to be snow on a nativity scene! Christmas and the birth of Jesus are in December, and there is snow! My mom would laugh at how silly we were. It does not snow in Bethlehem, she told us. My parents were able to see much of a world they otherwise would only dream of visiting had it been another time in history.

My dad trained in Kermine, Uzbekistan, Kirkuk, Iraq, Khanaqin, Syria, and in parts of Egypt before heading to Italy to fight the Germans. My mother was close by at a field hospital.

Dad's weekend and holiday passes

I imagine the excitement of seeing camels and donkeys in the streets, which were sights they witnessed, and hearing different languages being spoken, experiencing a mosaic of people and their cultures while traveling on their honeymoon, and while going from post to post. These experiences were momentous. The variety of the food alone would have made for a gastronomic adventure! Here were two people from Poland used to eating pierogi, smoked sausages, ham hocks, and cabbage with mushrooms. Now, they find themselves eating lamb, tabbouleh, tzatziki, and chickpeas with fragrant and exotic spices such as saffron, coriander, and cumin. My dad loved lamb and chickpeas and maybe this was when he developed a taste for them. Even if their trips were not glamorous, what they saw, the people they met, and the foods they ate, made this a once-in-a-lifetime experience.

While I was growing up, our family stayed close to home, spending summer vacations on small lakes in Western Pennsylvania to swim, fish, and relax. Aside from the fact that the family had limited financial resources, my parents did not like leaving home to travel. When I was older, I asked why they were reluctant travelers. The answer was that they had seen the world and traveled enough when they were young.

Chapter 26

The War Was Still Raging

During those war years when my parents were apart, there were letters and more letters exchanged about the usual pleasantries; asking what the other was doing, about how much they missed each other, and why he or she doesn't write more. Every so often, there were tidbits of information that told me more about what was really going on.

After the honeymoon, one of my mom's letters to dad revealed that mom was particularly melancholic. Since she had been so ill from typhus the year before, she experienced random and recurring illnesses. In one letter, she wrote about not feeling well and that she had received a letter from a person giving her information about her father. She, of course, did not write to dad about what she learned but said that when they were together again on leave, she would read the letter to him. Even though I know that my grandfather did not survive his exile in Siberia, knowing what she learned about his fate would have been enlightening and would have satisfied my curiosity.

Another letter from dad to mom—he talks about how he now saw her in a new and different light; how she is not the young girl he met in Kosów so long ago. After a weekend together, in the safety of my dad's presence, she broke down and went into a long tirade about the traumas and losses she experienced that were tearing her apart. Again, there were no details in the letter about what she said, but he mentioned how impressed he was with her strength. I can only guess that her outpouring may have recounted all the details of her imprisonments, the late-night interrogations, the mental torture, the disgusting physical conditions, the hunger and thirst, the long trip out of Siberia, mostly on foot, eating from the streets, her illness with typhus, the probable loss of her father, not knowing about her mother, and her fear for the future. With the war still raging and while working in the hospital, she witnessed severe injuries, diseases, mental trauma, and loss of hope. She was still young and newly married, but there was still much fear (today, her condition would be diagnosed as post-traumatic stress) in her life. Not often able to see her husband, she was also fearful for his safety.

Also, during this time, a few letters revealed that mom had some other physical problems. The deduction is that she may have suffered a miscarriage. She was trying to communicate the situation discreetly, mentioning a great deal of bleeding, and not being able to work her shifts due to weakness. She was very coy about the symptoms. Their letters were all censored at the time, which must be why she did not want to provide few details. Such an experience would have been mentally and physically burdensome, weighing heavily on her mind and spirit. There was more worry to come. The next stop was to be Italy—to fight the Nazis. The information about her vulnerable state comes as no surprise given what she had experienced in just over three years. But her resolve to remain strong was always the way she lived her life. While growing up, my mom was the glue that held the family together, the master mender of all that was broken. Her toughness and drive inspired us all.

Chapter 27

Fighting Back - The Italian Campaign

Their time together was limited and they were not even able to spend their first Christmas together. My dad's unit was still in Egypt while mom and the traveling hospital were in Port Said, near Tel Aviv, waiting for passage to Italy in December/January 1943–44. In January, my dad was transported to Italy. Once on Italian soil, the troops made their way north along the northern coast as the Polish Army. In 1943, the Allies invaded Sicily and then invaded the continent through the "toe." Shortly thereafter, Italy formally surrendered to the Allies, but Italy's surrender did not deter the Germans, who remained in control of Italy. At the time, the Allies were planning the invasion of Europe through France. President Roosevelt felt it was important to eliminate the German presence in Italy, which would also enable Allied naval forces to completely dominate the Mediterranean Sea, greatly improving communications with Egypt, the Far East, the Middle East, and India. In addition, it would mean that the Germans would have to transfer troops from the Eastern Front to defend Italian strongholds, which would help the Soviet Union advance from the East. Even without the Italians on their side, the Germans were a fighting foe in Italy. The first spring offensive in 1944 that involved the Polish Second Corps would be the Battle of Monte Cassino.

The Battle of Monte Cassino is also known as the Battle for Rome within the Italian Campaign. Since the Allies invaded the

Italian peninsula in 1943, the objective was to go north, capture Rome, and drive the Germans out of Italy. It was originally estimated that Rome would fall by October 1943, but that did not happen.

There were several gruesome and bloody battles that remain the worst of WWII, notably Anzio and Monte Cassino. Anzio proved to be a stalemate, with bloody battles raging from January to May 1944, while Monte Cassino, also called the Stalingrad of the Italian Front, was to be just as challenging and happening at the same time.

In the fall of 1943, the US Fifth Army successfully moved up the Italian "boot" after the fall of Naples. On the northeastern coast of Italy, the British Eighth Army was advancing up the Adriatic coast. The German Army was retreating north and established a defensive line called the Gustav Line in the middle of the "boot."

Before they established that line, the German Luftwaffe had seized control of the airfields of Foggia in September of 1943, even though the Allies signed an Armistice with Italy that same month. The Germans were determined to stop the advancing Allies even though Italy surrendered. Foggia is located on the north side of the peninsula, just north of the heel, east of Naples. By October, the United States Army Air Force and Royal Air Force bombed the airfields of Foggia, allowing the British 8th Army to seize control of the area a month later continuing the advancing Italian Campaign northward. The Polish Second Corps, then a part of the British 8th Army, was to see action soon and my dad was preparing.

As the Germans continued to retreat north, they found that there was a natural defensive line in the terrain which was provided by the Apennine Mountain, some of the roughest, wildest, and most remote terrain in the country. The Germans had been in this defensive position since the winter of 1943-44, holding the Gustav Line and regaining their strength since retreating from Northern Africa, Sicily, and Southern Italy.

While still in Foggia, prepared for the front, my dad corresponded with my mom. She was in nearby Palagiano, working at the field hospital. In April, he set out to see her, borrowing a buddy's motorcycle on a weekend pass. But after the motorcycle broke down, as he tells the story in a letter about this failed trip, he had to take an American transport back to his unit, grieving that he could not come to see her. Thinking that she was keeping him alive, he was holding a previous letter she wrote to him close to him at all times, reading and re-reading it. In it, she told him how scared she was that he was soon to be in battle and that she was having "silly" thoughts about his safety. In his letter to her written after the motorcycle incident, he said, "Quit your silly thoughts! Think only of the good times. What will be with me, will be." He said he would come back to her "when it is all over." Dad's unit was starting to see action, so he said they probably would not see each other for Easter. He was starting to see real bullets fly overhead. "No more fake training. At your hospital, they may be saying that all is still quiet on the front, but it's not true," he wrote. He warned her that letters would be more sporadic, because delivering supplies to the troops in the mountains was more important than delivering their letters. He wrote this letter in a foxhole and added that "I'll live. They won't kill everyone."

Many of these letters were deliberately vague for fear that censors would literally cut out compromising passages, as with all letters sent by mail. It was typical for the troops' letters to speak only in generalities, including pleasantries that were meticulously uninformative, avoiding anything specific or concrete about their lives. Earlier in the war, the censors were the Soviets. Now, it was the British Army making sure nothing compromising was being said about troop positions and activities. Sometimes, my parents were able to exchange unofficial letters delivered by an individual, which was done in all locations of the war. This way, letters did get through and the conversation could be more candid. For example, during this time in Italy, dad received a postcard from his sister who was still in Kazakhstan. The postcard was dated February 1943. It took thirteen months for this correspondence to find him. And how did it find him? These are the mysteries of the postal service in wartime. He asked mom to write back to Stasia, his sister.

Postcard from around the world

Within days of receiving the letter, dad was transferred to another unit which moved them to the rear. As a result, he was able to visit his wife for a couple of days after a long separation. She was in nearby Palagiano and their time together was perfect, but when it was time to leave, he thought to himself, "How can I leave?" He spoke about how hard it was for him to leave, expressing much regret and profound sadness and loss as he did so. These thoughts he shared in a letter after arriving back to his unit. They were feelings he had experienced for the first time. After previous visits with mom, he did not feel this burden. He wrote that now he was very afraid of what might happen. The reality of battle was setting in. Though he had been in battle before fighting in the September campaign in defense of Poland in 1939, it was different now. He had her.

Shortly thereafter, dad sent mom another letter, an action that he would later regret. That "bad" letter is nowhere in the collection of my mom's saved letters, but there are continuing references to this "evil" letter. Yet another letter followed immediately and it was an unofficial letter delivered to mom by a colleague of dad, in which dad wrote, "Please disregard the previous letter. I wrote it after having too many drinks and experienced some bad thoughts and feelings." He said the letter was written by a "madman." He also wrote that they "were going into battle soon, but please don't tell anyone, it's a secret." He described living on nerves and stress at all times. He also admitted that he was never afraid of dying until now; but now, he had someone to live for and she needed to know how frightening and treacherous his life was while preparing for battle.

At that moment, he was writing to her with artillery fire overhead, and yet he was calm, imagining her face as he remembered it from their days together in Kosów years before. Events had overwhelmed him before. Too many letters were not getting through the post in a timely fashion, and when he didn't receive a response from mom, it made him crazy and drove him to drink. He promised he would never write such a hateful letter again and he also promised to stop drinking.

The Battle for Monte Cassino was a long and challenging one for the Allies, lasting several months. This battle was critical in order to liberate Rome and continue the advance toward the north. The actual battle began in January 1944 with setbacks for both sides, and bloody stalemates were reminiscent of the trench warfare of World War I. Centered on the Gustav Line was the town of Cassino with its 6th Century Benedictine Monastery atop the hill. The area's terrain was filled with many deep underground bunkers and tunnels, with machine-gun emplacements, anti-tank ditches, and minefields, perfect for German defensive positions. Prior to the first attack on Cassino, the Allies were convinced that the Germans had troops and strategic defenses set up in the monastery, but had no proof. Being on the hill [Monte], the monastery was in an excellent position with its surrounding hills and valleys for German cover and artillery.

It took four major offensives between January and May 1944 before the line was eventually broken.[26]

The fourth and final battle was called "Operation Diadem," referencing a "crown" once worn by Oriental kings. It also indicated royal dignity or authority. This operation called for the U. S. Second Corps to attack up the coast toward Rome, the French

---

[26] Battle for Monte Cassino. The first unsuccessful battle for Monte Cassino took place in January 1944, involving the British X Corps, the US II Corps, the Moroccan-French troops, as well as the 2nd New Zealand Division and 4th Indian Division from the British 8th Army.

The second battle was called "Operation Avenger," which in some ways was a continuation of the first battle but now was complicated by logistical problems involving the 4th Indian Infantry Division. There were the issues of getting supplies to the troops on the ridges and valleys north of Cassino. They had to use mules crossing seven miles of goat tracks in full view of the monastery, subject to artillery fire. Operation Avenger did not breach the Gustav Line. High command was convinced at this point that the monastery must be bombed whether the Germans were in there or not.

The monastery was bombed in February 1944, making way for the Germans to occupy the rubble of the structure and set up defensive positions. Speculation about whether the Germans were there prior to the bombing did not matter. They were there now. The British Sussex Regiment was ordered to attack the Line. The fighting proved to be brutal, often hand-to-hand combat. The regiment lost over half its men. The Rajputana Rifles and the Gurkha Rifles joined the campaign. These regiments were from the 4th Indian Division. It was hoped that they would succeed because of their expertise in mountainous terrain, but progress was slow and their casualties heavy. The offensive failed.

The third battle started in mid-March in order to execute preliminary bombings after three weeks of bad weather. The bombings supported a ground assault by the British 78th Infantry Division under the command of the New Zealand Corps. New Zealanders and the Gurkhas were able to take a hill and a point, but at the same time, the Germans were able to reinforce their troops in the town while adding snipers to certain positions. Toward the end of March, the Allies planned to take both the town and the monastery, but the Germans counterattacked with the German 1st Parachute Division and what ground the Allies gained was lost. Both sides fought to exhaustion and suffered heavy casualties. The Allied line was reorganized and divisions replaced. Then, there was the fourth battle involving the Polish Second Corps. The Historical Eye.

www. historicaleye.com/WorldWar2/monte-cassino.html.

Corps to attack to their right, the British XIII Corps would be on the center-right, and to the right of the Brits fought the Polish Second Corps' 3rd and 5th Divisions commanded by Lt. General Władysław Anders. The Polish Army was now actively involved in fighting the German Army for the first time and my dad was in the light artillery regiment of the 5th Division. The men of the 3rd and 5th Divisions were largely formed by Polish exiles who had been deportees in Russia and Siberia from 1939 to 1941, as well as those who were imprisoned, exactly like my dad was.

Large troop movements took two months to put in place since they could only be done by moving small units at a time while creating diversions to maintain secrecy and the element of surprise. The Polish Army had relieved the 78th Division in the mountains behind Cassino, and would attempt to accomplish what the 4th Indian Division could not, which was to isolate the monastery and push around behind it into one of the valleys to link with the British XIII Corps and pinch out the Cassino position.

Two days before, the British 78th Division and XIII Corps were able to isolate Cassino from the valley; then on May 17, 1944, the Polish II Corps launched a second attack. The fighting was fierce with constant artillery and mortar fire. As their supply lines were threatened, the Germans withdrew from Cassino and retreated to form another defensive line further north called the Hitler Line. This pinching maneuver accomplished by the Polish and the British Corps was crucial to the overall success of the long battle. A patrol of the 12th Podolian Polish Cavalry Regiment made it to the summit of the mountain and raised a Polish flag over the ruins. Trumpeter, Oto Emil Czech, played the *Hajnał*, the "St. Mary's Call," over the ruins of the monastery after the Allied victory in the Battle of Monte Cassino. I would have loved for my dad to talk about this battle while he was alive, but somehow, I suspect he wouldn't have told me much. Many WWII veterans were very reluctant to discuss their wartime experiences, even with their families.

The Polish army lost over 1,000 soldiers while the total Allies' casualty count from all four segments of the battle was

55,000. At the foot of the Polish cemetery at Monte Cassino, there is an inscription in Polish dedicated to the soldiers who died in the battle which translates as:

> *Passerby, tell Poland that we fell faithfully in her service, for our freedom and yours, we Polish soldiers gave our souls to God, our bodies to the soil of Italy, and our hearts to Poland.*

My dad beat the odds. He survived.

Chapter 28

The Human Toll of War

My parents had only been married for seven months at the beginning of May 1944, when the Poles were brought in to fight the Germans. The Battle of Monte Cassino began, with only letters binding my parents together and now the stresses of war got the better of my dad. While under the influence of alcohol, dad wrote and sent a dreadful, hateful letter to mom. He admitted that he had too much to drink and had a hard time controlling himself when under stress. There were many apologies for the letter written by a "madman" as he called himself.

He had warned mom about letters not getting through in a timely manner, yet he fell into the trap of waiting and waiting for a letter from her and cursing her for not writing. This scenario had set the wheels in motion for the dreadful letter. The "makeup letter" admitted that he had not been afraid of dying until now, because now, she was the one he had to live for. The same problem of not hearing from dad plagued mom. She was worried about him, having not heard from him in days, and sometimes actually receiving letters out of chronological order. This worked out well for mom because she was prepared for the nasty letter since she had received the apology letter first. The misunderstanding was not just caused by waiting for letters but also by interpreting what was being said. Face-to-face conversations are different from writing a letter when one can't always explain details well enough or statements are taken out of context—especially when the letter is written during a stressful situation and under the influence of alcohol.

It's fascinating to see how a major military battle of World War II took second place to a marital squabble and how it played out in letters. At the same time, this exchange was wildly human, even though what I learned causes some uncomfortable feelings of being a voyeur regarding my parents' most intimate thoughts.

On the hospital side of the battle, mom saw many wounded being transported in for surgeries, amputations, infections, and in many cases, the last rites. Most of the time, she was so exhausted that she could hardly stand up. At the same time, she was very concerned about dad, knowing that she could not stay angry with him for long, knowing that he was in harm's way, frightened and stressed. She'd had wounded soldiers in her care who gave graphic details of what they experienced. They were from his unit so she knew the hell he and all the soldiers in his unit were going through. "With the grace of God, you will come back to me," she wrote, and "Stay strong to get through all this." She reported back to dad that one of his majors was on her floor and was doing well. Transports of wounded soldiers were coming in several times a day and night. But despite all the work, she was somehow holding up. "Don't worry about me," she wrote to dad.

Mom finally heard about my dad from an officer in his unit, reporting that dad was fine but that there were many wounded. Her prayers had been answered. Her Zdzich was safe, at least for now.

Letters were still not delivered in a timely fashion, even though mom wrote often. Dad reported to mom that he was proudly alcohol-free since May 8, which was her feast day. After the bad letter incident, it was now May 26. Even during the toughest time of the battle, which took place from May 11-17, he was alcohol-free. He went on to say that the Polish forces made their way into the monastery and found that the German paratroopers had already retreated and only found wounded German soldiers. The pressure was less but he was still losing hair as a result. She wrote back saying "If that is the only problem you have on the front, all is good. Come back to me, even if you are bald."

In the meantime, mom's own stress levels were increasing. "When will all this be over?" she kept wondering. She just wanted to scream and curse. "When can we begin to think and focus on each other and be together?" she would say aloud in anger. Even though the wounded count was decreasing, the war was not over. She continued to write often, providing dad some moral support and encouragement. He commented to her, "What is all the fuss? I'm ok." He felt this way until his unit came upon an area previously held by a German unit and found letters left behind by German soldiers who had received news from their loved ones. Those letters were written by supportive parents, wives, girlfriends, or siblings, the same kind of letters mom was writing to dad. The concept finally hit home for him—the universal concept of caring support and encouragement that a loved one can provide. Again, he had to apologize.

Both my parents survived the series of battles in Italy and for the Battle for Monte Cassino; they each received the Monte Cassino Commemorative Cross (*Krzyż Pamiątkowy Monte Cassin*). This medal was awarded to all soldiers of the Polish Second Corps who fought in the Battle of Monte Cassino. Mom was with the 3rd military hospital stationed at Palagiano. Her medal was #43031 and dog/ID tag # 1920-350-III. Dad fought in the 4 Pulk Artilerii Lekkie—(4th Light Anti-Aircraft Artillery Regiment of the 5th Kresowa Infantry Division). His award was number 19987 and dog/ID tag # 1916-286-III.

Letters from the Box in the Attic

All of mom's and dad's medals and mom's dog tags. The one encircled in the middle is mom's Monte Cassino Commemorative Cross awarded to all soldiers of the Polish Second Corps who fought. Mom's is #43031 for serving in the 3rd Military Hospital at Palagiano. The smaller one encircled to the right were her dog tags.

Disturbingly and unfortunately, dad's Monte Cassino medal and his dog tags were not saved, but there is documentation that he received the Monte Cassino Commemorative Cross.

Chapter 29

What was the Polish Army Fighting For?

After the Battle of Monte Cassino, Polish soldiers fought in other Allied battles to drive the German Army north and out of Italy. They, including my dad, were still in danger. There is a touching letter written in June of 1944, where Mom opens her heart to him. They had just spent six days together and she wrote, "I'm happy when you are happy." She went on to say that she believed they would have a solid, loving, and long marriage because he was worth it.

In July 1944, the Polish Second Corps was again victorious against the Germans by capturing the Port of Ancona along the Adriatic Sea, a battle in which my dad also fought. Shortly after this Battle, President Franklin Roosevelt wrote a citation honoring General Władysław Anders for "exceptional meritorious conduct, performing outstanding services to the United States and the Allied Nations" in the Italian Campaign. It was beneficial for the British 8th Army that Ancona was captured because the supply and communication lines were shortened. While the Polish Army was engaging in battle, the Western Allied leaders were making devastating decisions for Poland's future without consulting their Polish ally. Information was coming to light that in November 1943, Churchill, Roosevelt, and Stalin had met secretly in Tehran to discuss how to handle the "Polish problem." In essence, decisions were made to give Stalin the right to keep the land he annexed as a result of the Molotov-Ribbentrop Agreement between Germany and Russia in 1939 when Stalin was an enemy of Poland and the Allies.

As a result of the Tehran Conference in 1943, the Soviet Union was given the rights to her spoils for invading Poland in the first place. Poland was now fighting on the same side as the SSR and there was no protection from the United States and Britain— only concessions. Stalin desperately wanted and demanded a Soviet sphere of political influence in Eastern and Central Europe (specifically Poland). Stalin pledged to permit free elections in Poland "because the Russians had greatly sinned against Poland." In exchange for these concessions, Poland was to receive the promise of true independence for part of the country, not the Kresy, which was already in Stalin's hands. Poland was to receive new lands in the north and west at Germany's expense. My parents' homeland became the country that suffered the worst occupation in history, and by war's end had lost roughly six million citizens to mass murder and deportation at the hands of both Germany and Soviet Russia. She was worthy of full independence and certainly did not deserve to sacrifice a large portion of her land, especially to the Soviet Union, one of the original aggressors. The Polish Second Corps was primarily made up of soldiers who had been deported, imprisoned, and tortured by the Soviets. They had suffered tremendous personal losses and physical abuse, yet they fought valiantly alongside the Allies. The Kresy region was like a ping-pong ball during the war years, having been occupied by one or the other of the two aggressors. With Poland being invaded by the Nazis, and then the Soviets, the Kresy was then occupied by the Nazis again. Would that region now be given to the Soviets outright?

As a result of this secret conference and agreement among the three powers, my parents' homes would officially be no longer in Poland. What would happen to their families? Even though my mother probably had no immediate family left, she had uncles, aunts, and cousins.

When the Polish government pressed for assurances for this "true independence" as it was called, they received vague replies from Washington and London. The meeting in Tehran was to be *the first of three betrayals by the Western Allies* regarding Poland's future independence and land protection.

The opportunity to further Stalin's ultimate conquest of Poland came in August/September 1944. Since the war began, the Polish underground grew to 380,000 strong and became very effective in fighting the Nazis on Polish soil, engaging in many acts of sabotage. By 1944, it was the largest and strongest underground movement of any European country. Their primary effort was to carry out continuous resistance against the German occupation, receiving their orders from the High Command in London. By mid-1944, the Soviet Red Army was pushing the Germans out of the Soviet Union from the east into occupied Poland. While the Germans were suffering heavy losses in Italy and the Allied invasion had taken place in France, the question of a possible organized uprising in Poland was under consideration. An uprising in Warsaw against the Germans would help the Russians advance into Poland and on to liberate Warsaw. This would be a precursor to advancing into Germany and ultimately liberating and occupying Berlin. It was thought that the only way to push the Germans out of Warsaw was if the Polish underground in Warsaw received help from the Soviet Union.

Many in command like General Anders knew that Russia's intentions were solely self-serving and should not be trusted. Nevertheless, the Polish Cabinet exiled in London authorized the uprising in Warsaw by the Home Army (*Armia Krajowa*), made up of 40,000 men and women soldiers on active service within Warsaw's borders. After the first day of battle, the Polish underground was able to seize most of the capital city. Their battle cry was "Poland is fighting, Poland will live, Poland will overcome."

However, after a few weeks, the tide turned in their quest for final victory. While the underground command pleaded for help from the Allies, the Red Army was sitting across the Wisła River, not willing to help. The Home Army commander sent a scathing telegram to the Polish Government in London describing the lack of defense against the German Army and pleading for help from the Allies. He said, "I state that Warsaw in her struggle receives no assistance from the Allies, just as Poland received none in 1939 (referring to the Phony War). The balance sheet of our alliance with Great Britain so far shows only our assistance in 1940 in the defense of the British Isles, in the Norwegian campaign, in Africa, Italy, and on the western front. We demand that you clearly state this fact to the British..." The scathing plea went on and on.[27]

The support given to the Allies by Polish soldiers refers to those who were able to escape to neutral countries and found their way to France and Britain after the September Campaign of 1939. They then were able to fight the Germans in the west. From 1939 to 1944, Polish airmen, infantry, and sailors, after escaping to the west, fought in all the Allied campaigns, not just in Italy.

Help was attempted under British command. Several sorties flown by Polish airmen in the RAF made efforts to deliver arms and ammunition to Warsaw but they were shot down by the Germans. The American Army Air Force was prepared to drop equipment and supplies into Warsaw and proposed the aircraft land on American bases in Soviet Russia for refueling, but Stalin refused to grant permission. As usual, Poland received no support because Stalin influenced the decision once again.

Meanwhile in Italy, the Polish Second Corps was still engaged in battles along the Adriatic coast. After Ancona, the 5th (Kresy) Division, my dad's division, was involved in the Battle of Metauro, which was the heaviest in the Adriatic sector.

Toward the end of August 1944, General Anders had a "sit down" conversation with Winston Churchill. Mr. Churchill was of course very flattering to the General about Polish accomplishments, but he was concerned about the morale of the Polish soldiers. General Anders said that each soldier was first and foremost

---

[27] Home Army commander's plea for help - General Bor-Komorowski's telegram: *An Army in Exile,* by General Władysław Anders, page 203

obligated to the task of destroying the Germans, but at the same time, the soldiers were concerned about the future destiny of their country and the events in Warsaw. After some political posturing, Churchill pleaded that General Anders should "trust Great Britain, who will never abandon you, never." General Anders responded that categorically, Poland would never consent to the Russians taking as much territory as they wished. They would never consent to such a *fait accompli* and that all discussions about future boundaries should be done at the peace table after the war.

From August 1 to October 5, 1944, the Polish underground resistance organization in Warsaw fought valiantly but eventually capitulated to the Germans. Those who survived two months of battle were treated as prisoners of war and sent to German prison camps. The Germans completely destroyed the city to expedite the underground army's surrender, while all along, the Red Army, sitting on the other side of the river, intended to come into the city only after surrender took place. It was always Stalin's intent to have the Red Army liberate Warsaw and the Polish people.

My reflection on these events, after reading General Anders' book, *An Army in Exile*, is one of great anger and pain. Soldiers fight for country, freedom, honor; but for the Polish soldier, his country was being used as leverage, a negotiating tool, primarily to have the Soviets declare war on Japan. The feeling that they were being disrespected was demoralizing for the Polish troops who were still engaged in battle. But there was still a small glimmer of hope that their country would emerge free after the war, and their lands not be taken. There was no *fait accompli,* not yet, not officially.

Chapter 30

Fait Accomplis' and its Consequences - The Ultimate Betrayal

"Fait Accompli" is a phrase originating from the French language, literally meaning "accomplished fact," but more specifically, "something that has already happened or been decided before those affected hear about it, leaving them with no option but to accept." Poland's fear of losing its eastern borderlands to the Soviets was becoming a reality, and they would have no option but to accept.

The second of three betrayals by the Western Allies happened as news broke of the Yalta Conference in February 1945. Churchill, Roosevelt, and Stalin were known as the "Big Three." They decided that Germany was to be disarmed and divided into four occupation zones; eastern Polish borders were to be set to the advantage of the Soviets, and **Soviet Russia pledged to hold free elections in Eastern Europe.**

The decisions about the eastern borderlands being handed to Stalin dealt the Polish soldiers of the Second Corps a crushing blow. What they all feared was going to happen did. The homes in the Kresy, my parents' hometowns, would now officially no longer be in Poland.

General Anders sent a telegram to the President of the Polish Republic in Exile and a letter to the commanding general of the British Eighth Army in essence saying that he, Anders, "cannot in good conscience continue to put his soldiers in harm's way and expect additional sacrifices from them when the three powers unilaterally decided to surrender the eastern territories of Poland to the Soviets." The gross injustice is that this region was invaded by the Soviets in 1939 and thousands of its inhabitants were arrested and deported into Siberia. The other galling but heroic fact was that the majority of the soldiers in the Second Corps were from the region in question. They in fact were victimized by the Soviets, and now, they could no longer call their home Poland.

Even under those dire circumstances, General Anders, the consummate soldier, assured the British command that he would never abandon the Eighth Army by putting them in jeopardy with his refusal to fight. But at the same time, how could he answer his soldiers when asked why they should continue to shed their blood?

The Polish Government in London made the decision to continue to fight side by side with the Allies against Germany until final victory. At this time, General Anders was appointed acting Commander-in-Chief of all Polish Armed Forces because the general who was to be named as head of the army was sitting in a German POW Camp following the failed Warsaw Uprising. General Anders made a long public statement to his troops, commending them for their sacrifices in all battles and how they had upheld the honor of their country. His final directive to his soldiers was if anyone asked them "What are you fighting for?" "Answer them," he said, "that the Polish soldier is fighting today for the same ideal for which he went to war five years ago: ***to prevent, in our country and in the whole world, might prevailing over right.***"[28]

Another worrisome situation at that particular time was that all of Poland had now been liberated by the Red Army.

On the world stage, the Polish Government in Exile in London tried to engage Stalin to discuss future peacetime neighborly relations between two sovereign nations that share a border. With

---

[28] "To prevent in our country and in the whole world, might prevailing over right."—Anders Quote delivered in a speech to his troops. *Army in Exile*, by General Władysław Anders, pages 261-262.

that gesture, Moscow delivered a statement regarding an agreement that Stalin had signed with the communist puppet government in Warsaw, which he had put in place, rejecting the authority of the legitimate and free Polish government in London.

By this time, the war finally came to an end in Europe on May 8, 1945, but all the suffering and misery was not over for millions in war-torn Europe. It had to be a great day of celebration for all the Allied troops to have the war behind them. Now the process of picking up the pieces of their lives needed to begin.

The third betrayal of Poland by the Western Allies took place at the Potsdam Peace Conference in July 1945. The "Big Three" decided that the German people residing in Czechoslovakia, Hungary, and Poland were to be repatriated back to Germany and Germany's boundaries were to be adjusted. And oh, by the way, there would be no free elections in Poland or any part of Eastern Europe, permanently subjugating the residents to communism. This information was delivered by none other than Joseph Stalin.

Potsdam was the final blow to the Polish people all over the world, who viewed these decisions simply as appeasing Stalin. Polish territory was lost to the Soviets, and with no free elections, there was no hope of having an independent nation.

Poland had feared it would lose its eastern borderlands but now, the entire country was lost to repressive rule. With no independence in their future, it was a *fait accompli*. There was no V-E Day for Poland. Tracing the discourse back to the Yalta Conference, the Polish fate was sealed. The "Big Three" sold out Poland and the Polish people to the Soviets despite Churchill's promises. During the war, the Poles repeatedly heard German propaganda that one day, Poland would be handed to Soviet Russia. The propaganda was now the truth.[29]

In addition to these betrayals, there was the humiliation the Polish soldiers experienced. They were victorious in battle against the Germans but lost the battle for their homeland. The British Government refused to allow the free Polish Army to march in the

---

[29] *An Army in Exile*, by General Władysław Anders, page 253.

formal victory parade in London in June 1946. The staunchly anti-communist Polish soldiers were prevented from participating in the Allied victory celebration. The British government feared that it would offend Stalin and the puppet government in Warsaw; thus, they left out all the fighting Poles.[30] Poland would now be ruled by a communist government, suffering under another oppressor, worse by some accounts than what the country had suffered under German oppression. At this time, there were a million displaced Polish citizens scattered all over the world and the majority did not want to return to Poland and its repressive conditions. After all, they fought for freedom, not repression; and they, including my parents, did not want to return to dictatorial conditions. In fact, young Polish men, many of who were coming of age during that time, were leaving their country to avoid deportation to Siberia or worse, possibly even execution, because they may disagree with the new Communist regime. Many were leaving Poland, while the majority of those displaced refused to return.

For a while, the official British position was that all Polish soldiers should repatriate to Poland following the end of the war, despite the new regime that was forming in Warsaw and despite their future safety being in jeopardy. My parents had definitely decided not to go back to Poland for fear of re-arrest, which was happening to others who did return. Those who dared return and who had been found to be enemies of Mother Russia during the early years of war were being re-arrested. Why would they risk their personal safety to go back? Those who fought for a free Poland were deemed "traitors" by the communist regime. So now what? Where would they go? Were they doomed to be "DPs" [displaced persons] or refugees forever in exile? Another problem was that my parents were still in Italy; still in the army at the end of the war and now it was 1946.

For the soldiers and support staff of the Polish Second Corps in Italy, it was now a year since the war ended and they had not yet demobilized. Since my parents and close to 100,000 soldiers

---

[30] *An Army in Exile*, by General Władysław Anders, pages 265-270.

had nowhere to go, General Anders insisted that they remain together. He wanted someone, some country, to take responsibility for his army, the army that had served so valiantly. After all, they had fought with the Allies for world freedom and now there was no free country that would have them. The good news was that after many discussions between General Anders and the British Government, it was agreed that no one would be forced to repatriate to Communist Poland against their will. Great Britain, after much time but to her credit, was the only Allied country to realize that there was a moral obligation to the Polish soldiers who fought so long and hard side by side with the Allies. They would help those who feared to return to their homeland. A year after the end of World War II, the order came down from London that the Polish Armed Forces were to be transported to Great Britain for demobilization.

Mom got this news of their pending transport to England and described it as news that caused a panic. Everyone in mom's and dad's units had been leading comfortable lives in Italy while their fates were in limbo. Just days before, they wrote to each other saying they needed to schedule time off together to do some sightseeing and relaxing, and now, they did not know when they would see each other again and when each would be transported out of Italy. My mother expressed her desire to stay in Italy and not go to England since there was news that in England, there were hardships of poverty and rationing.

It was decided they needed to go where the army was sending them if they were ever to have a civilian life together. By the beginning of June, mom received word that she and her hospital were one of the first to be transported to Britain and they were scheduled to leave by the middle of July. My parents' letters talked about what they should buy while still in Italy for fear of the scarcity of goods in England. Mom had been able to have a couple of dresses tailored over the last several months, but if she bought fabric now, there would not be time to have a dress made. They discussed having a ring remade since it would hold its value, fearing the value of the currency may plummet. She mostly wrote about how much it pained her to leave and to leave her Zdzich behind because it was uncertain when he would be traveling to England.

Her transport set sail on July 21, 1946. The passage took them by way of the Straits of Gibraltar and Spain, north to the British Isles, over rough waters, making many of them sick for much of the passage. Each day was an adventure and a new experience. Many of her fellow nurses were interested in escaping their uniform trappings.

Permission was given for the women to wear stylish dresses if they desired while going out to party each night. They wanted to take advantage of their freedom while onboard a cruise ship. Even though they were allowed to wear civilian clothes, mom felt that pulling out an ironing board and getting all dressed up was too much work. She and her good friend Wanda, two married girls, would go to the cinema, see several movies while onboard ship, socialize with some Brits, and try to become acclimated to the new language that they would need to learn.

The passage took six days, and by then, they were ready to get off the high seas and on solid dry land. Port of Call was Liverpool, which she found quite lovely on a warm sunny day when they disembarked. The predicted daily rain did not find them in Liverpool which was refreshing. Their first introduction to England after going through customs was the need to find and use a washroom. What they found was a pay toilet. What was that all about to cost one pence? Never seeing such a thing, they figured out that by holding the door of the stall open, they were able to get their whole transport in and out of the washroom without any problem—and all for just one pence!

They took a train and then a bus to a camp, their new home. By the next day, their luggage was efficiently delivered to them. The countryside was lush with vegetation and the town of Buckden outside of Diddington Camp, Huntingdonshire was populated by charming little houses dressed with flowers, just like Emma and Zdzich had dreamed about having one day for themselves. This new area was where the 6th Polish Hospital and camp was to be.

Within days, the sick and wounded arrived, glad to see their nurses. All the stories they had heard about imposed rationing were true. Mom had warned my dad that the food was not very good either and the bad food was being rationed. As with all shortages of goods, there was a criminal element that sought to circumvent the system.

Mom reported to dad that ration coupons were available on the black market as well as forgeries, but that the British police arrested and prosecuted both the buyers and the sellers of forgeries. So "you should buy some salami before you set sail because you can't get any here." And "buy fabric for a new suit and have it made."

She explained also to buy anything else he needed in Italy because it takes eight months to get a new pair of pants in England. "Stores in town have beautiful window displays but you can't actually buy anything." Also, she suggested he have some loose change with him when he arrives in port and goes through customs in case he needed to use a washroom! Her most serious words recalled that just three weeks ago, they had a leave together, had their last meals and walks together, but now, they were still far from each other and needed to correspond by letter.

Her new living arrangements were not very comfortable, which were unlike what she had experienced over the last two years in Italy.

Previously, she either roomed with one other person or had her own room. Now she had to live in a barracks housing six women, where privacy was at a premium. There were six beds and one desk in a space which should have comfortably accommodated one or two people. The noise and the distractions, the singing and the chatter, were too much when she was used to peace and quiet. She had to adopt a similar mindset as she did when in Soviet Russia. "I have to make myself get used to it," she wrote.

By October 1946, my dad's unit was one of the last to leave Italy en route to England. His camp would be in Circencester, about 100 miles from where mom was stationed in Diddington.

How much longer would they have to wait before they could actually live as husband and wife under one roof?

This was the beginning of my parents' lives in the west, residing in Great Britain as of 1946. Ironically, in that same year, my grandparents and aunt were repatriated to Poland from Kazakhstan, not to their former territory in the east, which was no longer Poland. They were resettled in former German territory in June 1946, a territory that became a part of the new Poland. Massive migrations of both Polish and German citizens were taking place as both groups were being forcibly resettled in new towns once again. The Germans living in Polish territory had to migrate back to Germany, while Poles leaving Siberia and other parts of Poland were to be resettled in former German land or in areas of Poland. This was all authorized by the three powers. The Brits and the Americans appeased Stalin by allowing him to keep the Eastern part of Poland; thus, creating the need to open up new territory for Poland at Germany's expense. But what they also wanted to accomplish was to create ethnically homogeneous boundaries for nations coming out of World War II, which was not done after World War I.

In my opinion, the United States, because it is a melting pot of ethnicities, does not really understand nationalism on the same level as it exists in Europe; the kind that has influenced attitudes and caused wars over the centuries. However, within our own borders, in 2018, we do know about racial and religious tensions, which have a similar foundation. Because of today's global society, fear of certain ethnicities and religions has created tensions and tragedies. As a human race, because we bow to human nature, too often we are not tolerant of people who are different from we are.

The timing of the resettlements is a sad testament to the realities of war. People caught in the fighting are being positioned and re-positioned like pawns on a chessboard. The aftermath of war has as many devastating consequences as did the war itself.

Whether one is a civilian or a soldier now needing to create a new life devoid of war, with or without family, what does one do? How does one acclimate? After all the movement my parents had to endure, now, there was yet another new country to call home, Great Britain. During that time, my grandparents and aunt were repatriated to Gliwice, Poland where there were many shortages of goods and services, creating the need for families to rely on the goodness of others.

Chapter 31

Poles Scattered All Over the World

Polish men, women, and children had been victimized because of the deportations and as a result, they were left scattered all over the world. How did they get to Australia, New Zealand, Africa, and India?

When the new Polish Army was leaving the Soviet Union, the civilians followed hoping to be fed and feel safe. Those who survived the journey out of the Soviet Union required care and housing, especially the children. During the war, many civilian refugee camps were set up, but that was not a permanent solution since they were primarily transient camps and were not self-sustaining. A more permanent solution was offered by the British government. They set up transport to countries within their Commonwealth of Nations where permanent camps were created for refugee families and orphaned children. During the war years, many Poles found themselves in the care of India, Africa, Australia, New Zealand, and even Mexico. At that time, the United States was not willing to accept any refugees, but the president of Mexico did, providing a camp outside of Mexico City, mostly for orphaned children.

Other Poles, like dad's family who could not get out of the Soviet Union, waited until the end of the war to find out if they could be repatriated to Poland or whether they had to remain Soviet citizens. My dad had not heard anything from his family in Kazakhstan since receiving a postcard in January 1943. Stalin cut diplomatic relations with the Polish Government in Exile in London in spring 1943 after the Katyń murders were discovered and made public. Letters stopped coming out of the Soviet Union, since Poland blamed Stalin for the atrocities. My dad heard from an old friend from Stryj, his Polish hometown, that his family was resettled in Gliwice, formerly Gleiwitz of Upper Silesia of the Third Reich. Many Poles formerly from dad's area were settled in that part of the new Poland. It took my dad's family, my grandparents, and my aunt seven weeks and 7,000 kilometers or over 4,300 miles to travel out of the steppes of Kazakhstan to arrive in Gliwice in June 1946. In February of that year, my mom received a letter from a person in Switzerland who told her that people from Kosów were being resettled in the same region as dad's family, although not the same town. She immediately thought that she would hear from her mother soon.

The fog of war was slowly lifting as people were coming out of the woodwork, revealing themselves, looking for loved ones, needing to start their lives over. People were exchanging information about friends, family members, and total strangers. The first post-war letter my dad received from his family was in September of 1946. Dad's family heard from a friend from Stryj that dad had married his pre-war girlfriend and that the couple had miraculously found each other during the war. Dad's sister wrote, "I thought they were meant to be with each other." In that letter, dad's sister, Stasia, mentioned that she had corresponded with mom's mother, Magdalena, until June of 1941, but then lost contact with her. Magdalena even sent them a package from Kosów trying to help them out during the time they were in Kazakhstan. Stasia wrote that she would try to find out what happened to my grandmother.

That September letter was catch-up time between dad and his family, trying to account for four years of their lives wasted in Siberia since their last correspondence. What they went through, Stasia wrote, was too painful to talk about. The sheer fact that they survived the ordeal and made it out of the Soviet Union was a miracle. But now, they had literally nothing. When they arrived in

Gliwice, they stayed with Adam's family for a few months until an apartment became available. They also received some help from another old friend from Stryj. Families tried to help each other as each came in out of the cold. Dad's family, all three of them, contracted malaria in Kazakhstan. The disease followed them to Poland since it has a way of recurring and medicines were scarce. Stasia felt extremely lucky to get a job doing office work, so even though she was ill, she needed to keep her job by showing up to work to get paid. Grandfather got a job as a railroad repair shop mechanic, similar to what he did before the war in Stryj. In this letter, Stasia became very melancholic when she wrote to my dad sarcastically, "Imagine, in pre-war Stryj, walking the streets in torn and tattered clothes." She vowed that it would get better for them; their lives had to improve.

Her focus had always been on their mother and keeping her healthy. They were everything to each other while in exile and they each made sure the other would survive Siberia. She went on to write that at age 34, "I feel like an old lady, and not knowing the fate of Adam only makes me feel older. After six years of hard labor, starvation, and poverty in Siberia, I was almost destroyed."

My dad wrote to his sister about what he had learned while in Palestine, about the massacre in Katyń, and that he saw a posting of the names of the Katyń victims. Her husband Adam's name was on the list. Receiving this information, she wept, unwilling to accept this information as an outcome. "Who put the list together?" she asked in a return letter. "Were there birthdates shown and hometowns listed or just names?" I have to believe that deep down inside, she knew all along that he was dead, but now, getting closer to the truth was more than she could bear. In a subsequent letter, she asked my dad if he could help her get a death certificate for him.

When I was growing up, my mom did talk about Ciocia Stasia's husband, about Adam being murdered by the Soviets, but never referred to Katyń as the name for this massacre, or what that event meant to them as a family or to Poland as a nation. These letters between dad and his sister along with what I've learned about this subject put a name and a face to this tragic event. It all made sense when I learned the details of the Katyń massacre and about what I know of Adam's murder.

There were angry letters to my dad from his sister when he did not write back quickly enough. In her desperation, she wrote, "After all, we need so much; we get no social aid and desperately need malaria medicine." She apparently did not realize or care that dad's unit was still in Italy and he was about to be transported to Britain for demobilization. There was not much he could do for them until he was on British soil. It was now the beginning of November 1946. Their mother was sick with malaria again and needed medicine, a warm dress, and a coat as the days were getting colder. Stasia wrote that she would kill herself if it were not for their mother "who needs me and if I did kill myself, our mother could not handle such a tragedy." With lives disrupted and nearly destroyed by violence and death, the loss of hope can be just as harmful. Without Adam, she felt that her future was dismal, but what saved her was having her mother's warmth and love at her side as she wrote. These were desperate times for so many who were trying to find a way to put their lives back together.

For a while, Polish radio, broadcast in Poland only, provided a service where people could submit lists of family members' names to be read on the air in the hope of finding relatives and friends. However, that service ceased shortly after it started. Nevertheless, family members eventually were able to find information about loved ones either through the International Red Cross or through the help of friends and total strangers. Dad's mother learned from others about the fate of her sister Maria and her husband and their daughter Janka. Maria's husband had to stay behind in Russia after amnesty and died, and at the time, Ciocia Maria did not know the real details of his death. Dad's mom learned that her sister's husband committed suicide while still in the Soviet Union. The three of them were preparing to leave Kazakhstan after amnesty and had just received their travel documents. Ciocia's husband was robbed of his papers and told his wife and daughter to go on without him, while he looked into replacing them. That task apparently was not easy as the Soviets were making it difficult for the Poles to leave their enslavement. He felt helpless and trapped and then became very despondent about his situation, ending his life by jumping in front of a train. The story that Ciocia Maria had heard from a friend, shortly after the incident, was that her husband fell ill and died.

The letters continued to reveal tragedies as family members learned about their loved ones. Dad's cousin, Janka's husband, had been a POW, first in Hungary then was shipped to Germany until the end of the war. After the war, Janka and her mother were stranded in Beirut, Lebanon and after Janka's husband was released from the German POW camp, he returned to Poland. He reached out to his young wife asking her to return to Poland, but she and her mother could not do so. Upon returning to Poland, her husband met someone else and started a family. During the war, Janka had planned to travel to Africa or India but never did. After the war, she wrote about wanting to go to Australia, but both she and her mother reached out to my dad for help to get them the right papers to immigrate to England. In 1949, they finally made it, nine years after being deported to Siberia.

In 1946, my parents tried to adjust to their life in England, although it was complicated by having family so far away with their own living situation in flux. My dad was stationed in a camp west of London and my mother worked at a hospital north of London. A transfer for mom brought them closer but it was not until the following year when they actually set up a household together, in Chandlers Ford, southwest of London after four years of marriage.

My dad's official job after serving in the military was as a driver for the Polish Resettlement Corps. Post-war supplies and jobs were scarce, and the economic conditions in all the European nations were desperate. Economies were exhausted, poverty was rampant, industrial production was low, and millions were homeless. As an added hardship, there was much anti-Polish sentiment in England which began during the war and continued after it ended. Great Britain hosted thousands of people from different countries for five years, and by 1946, the British people were eager to see them leave. The country suffered shortages of everything, from ladies' underwear to food and fuel. Not enough people understood why some of these foreigners, particularly the Polish, did not want to or could not go home.

The Resettlement Corps was created to help Polish soldiers and their families transition into civilian life in Great Britain, while still having the contractual structure and discipline of the military.

The Corps helped them find employment or training to increase their chances of finding suitable civilian life employment. My dad had filled out a questionnaire in 1946 while still in Italy, which asked about his interests and previous education and training. This information then fed into the resettlement program. He had given them his prewar education, employment history, and other interests. This was something I learned from digging into his military records.

Much to my surprise, I learned that dad had been a property insurance adjuster and underwriter before the war. I had been a casualty claims adjuster for a while post-college. We had something in common, but he never talked about his former career while I was working in the industry. Also, he had been a skier as well as a ski instructor and a horseback riding instructor. I never knew any of this about my father! His other avocations as listed in the questionnaire were interests in agriculture and farming, including taking care of animals. Mentioning agriculture did not come as a surprise to me. When he and my mom bought their house in Sewickley, they had a garden that was tiny by many standards but produced an enormous quantity of fruits and vegetables. My husband Alan lovingly referred to their backyard as the "South 40" [acres]. They grew many vegetables such as pole beans, tomatoes, cucumbers, kohlrabi, Brussel sprouts, and herbs and had cherry, apple, and peach trees. My dad also indicated that if retraining was available, he would be interested in precision metalwork and/ or welding. He had welded in Lithuania for a year at the sugar factory. Eventually, he welded for a living at American Bridge, a steel mill in the United States.

Because the Poles were seen as competition for some of the British trade unions, anti-Polish sentiment spread, which further turned public opinion against them. This sentiment was enough for my father to conclude that it was time to leave the island nation. His top three choices were to go to the United States first, then Canada, and then New Zealand. There were opportunities for passage to these and other nations with financial help from the British government. My parents began talking about going either to Argentina with mom's friend Wanda and her husband or to the United States where my parents each had a distant uncle. The Corps dissolved in 1949 and my father was officially discharged from the Army/Resettlement Corps on April 1, 1949.

Chapter 32

Desperate Times

Letters continued between Poland and England with fervor. My dad's parents and sister were very grateful for all the packages that they continued to receive from England. There were guidelines to follow when sending a package to prevent its contents from being stolen. If one was sending a pair of shoes, one was required to send one package with the left shoe and another package with the right shoe. The declaration form indicated the contents of the package and shoes would qualify as valuable, potentially to be stolen. From Poland, there were frequent requests for cloth to make dresses and coats, fur or blankets to line coats for warmth, dress pants, hats, eye drops, malaria medicine, leather to re-sole shoes, or to have a new pair made. My grandmother was a seamstress and could create something from just about anything. She asked for used clothes—"bigger is better" she said because she could remake them to fit. She asked for eye drops because of her recurring bouts with malaria; she was weakened and often couldn't see at night when she needed to sew. Time spent sewing and mending for others was a source of extra income for the family, in addition to what she created for her daughter, herself, and husband. She could ill afford to lose time because her eyes were failing at night.

Some of these letters were gloomy while hopeful, especially the one my parents received at Christmas time in 1946. Dad's parents and sister sent their Christmas greetings with the hope that next year, things would be different. The letter recounted how they all cried while sitting at their Christmas Eve dinner table, remembering Christmas in 1938, their last Christmas together before the world changed. Next year, in 1947, they dreamed that they would all be together again, sitting around the Christmas Eve table along with other friends who were thrown out of their homes and displaced. Dad's mom was very sweet in her letters to my mother describing how pleased she was that my mom was making her son so happy, since "he lost the warmth of his family during the war." Officially, the Christmas of 1946 was the first post-war Christmas for all of them following their return to Poland from Kazakhstan until June of 1946, while my parents were in Britain by the end of 1946. The rest of the European world saw an end to hostilities in May of 1945, which made for a celebratory Christmas that December; but unfortunately, for many displaced Poles, their war did not end until much later.

A letter received in January 1947 was from Stasia describing her extreme sadness. She spent much time crying now after returning to her homeland. She was now able to finally relax and let the tears flow, she wrote, after so many years of being strong, "hard as a rock," as she described herself, for herself and their mother. Finally, the many years of harsh suffering and demanding physical labor were over. "Six years of hard knocks in Siberia nearly destroyed me," she wrote. "I am no longer the happy, lighthearted person I was in the pre-war years," she went on to say. Still suffering from the loss of her husband, she vowed never to marry again, and she never did. Many of her girlfriends were getting married, and this depressed her; but she did start to warm to the idea that she was a lovable person, unlike how she perceived herself during her years in exile when mistrust and lies were part of her life. She admitted that she was starting to feel better about her life and was feeling "human" again.

News from my mother's family was starting to emerge. Uncle Franek was busy rebuilding several churches, driving his horse-drawn buggy from one parish to another. Other letters revealed that extended family members were arriving from the East and being resettled in a region called Silesia, "Śląsk" in Polish. Stasia wrote that she would travel to meet and visit mom's family.

The wartime story had now come full circle from the perspective of family members being reunited, either by knowledge or what happened to them or where they actually were.

But there is so much more to the story. What happens to people who come out of a war experience and all of a sudden need to blend into society? Do they spend the rest of their lives fighting off their demons? And how do they do it? I need to share my sentiments about those post years.

Chapter 33

Introspection

Several letters revealed family dynamics that I had never knew. While growing up, personal human failings were never talked about in my family. Mom would say, "If you have nothing good to say about a person, don't say anything at all." A few letters here and there revealed the fact that my grandfather, dad's father, was not always a nice person. He was a bit of a tyrant and ruled the household in a gruff manner. In a post-war letter, my dad asked his father whether he was still drinking and if his dad remembered the promise he made when dad was going off to war. The promise was that my grandfather would treat his wife well, or at least better than he usually did. The letters in response were from all parties: my grandmother, my aunt, and from my grandfather himself noting that he was trying to be kinder and more sensitive. Apparently, my grandfather did have a drinking problem. Before the war, he would go out with his friends from town, drink too much, and get very angry about something. This resulted in his throwing his weight around once he got home. Post-war letters go on to say that since some of his friends from Stryj were living nearby, he would still go out, but not drink as much. He confessed that it was because he just didn't have enough money. Dad's sister would write about her father and did not mince words when referring to his drinking. In the one letter when she spoke about how she wanted to end her life, the only mention of her dad was that Stasia "honors him" as her father, but otherwise, she wrote, "He is dead to me. What he was like before the war, he's the same if not worse now." For peace and quiet, she tolerated him.

As dad's family in Poland started to get back on their feet, they did not need as much help from England anymore. However, in a letter from the summer of 1947, my grandfather asked my parents for a new suit, as he only had his work clothes. My grandfather had always been a sharp dresser, so not having good dress clothes was probably a hardship for him. Grandfather admitted that the suit did not have to be new; secondhand was fine. After receiving the suit, he thanked my dad for the beautiful suit. "It fits perfectly and to my taste," he wrote. He also asked for a lightweight coat, and my dad agreed to send him one only if grandfather again promised to be good to his wife and daughter. In response, grandfather wrote that he was trying to be a better person, but sometimes, "Life gets in the way."

Even though my dad was concerned about his father's drinking habits and behavior, my dad also had a love for the bottle. After my parents were engaged, he would write my mother about how much he missed her, and then he would go to the bar and drown his feelings in the drink because they were not together or she wasn't writing enough. It seems to me that the difference between my dad and his own father was that my grandfather went out with friends, but my dad stayed at camp and drank alone in his tent or went to the bars alone. After dad's engagement, his buddies stopped inviting him out because all he talked about was his fiancée and how much he loved and missed her. From what I heard, my dad used to be very social. There are reprimands in his military record for being a rabble-rouser and partying too much, but not after he got engaged, and certainly, not after he got married. If he did not hear from mom often enough, he would worry and brood, then drink too much, and then trouble happened, like the time just prior to the Battle of Monte Casino, where a simple misunderstanding blew into a negative situation, all due to alcohol. This type of behavior carried on into his civilian life.

It is said that "The apple does not fall far from the tree," which could be accurate when referring to my dad following his father's footsteps. I never knew my grandfather, but I don't think that statement creates the complete picture. Both father and son could have had the same issues, but the way I looked at my dad was that when he drank, he was depressed or sad. Grandfather was probably depressed and sad too but would party. According to the letters, he would do this even when there was not enough money; he wanted to go out with friends to blow off some steam. I do not remember my dad ever drinking the rent money away or going out with friends to have fun.

I remember one occasion on a Friday or Saturday night when dad drank at home and then he and I went for a walk around town. I was at least fifteen or sixteen years old because I had either a permit or my driver's license. We walked past the local Chevy dealer in town and looked at a new Camaro. Dad talked to the salesman and said he wanted to get his daughter a car. Well, that was a fun conversation to hear! The next day, the phone kept ringing when the salesman tried to follow up on his new lead. Dad got so angry about the salesman's calls and refused to speak to the salesman. I was not delusional about getting a car, but for a few seconds, the idea was exciting to contemplate. On other occasions, he would shout abusive words at my mother for no apparent reason, targeting her, maybe making himself feel better while making her feel that she was the cause of all his problems. This I witnessed several times as a preteen and teen, seeing my mother crying in her sewing room after an alcohol-induced argument. I was still young but even then, I would ask my mom, "Why don't you leave? You don't have to put up with this!" Her answer was always "But where would I go?" The next day, he would feel bad and would apologize, but my mom would hold that fear and abuse close to her heart. Each time, it would take her a while to fully forgive him. It appears that this kind of drinking and abusive anger was similar in both grandfather and dad.

Many dads are special people and my dad was in that group. I was like many daughters; we worship our dads growing up. They are our first "boyfriends" as little girls. Dads are our knights in shining armor, family protectors, usually family breadwinners and sweet men whom daughters can influence with a smile or a tear. The words *mój tatuś* means 'my daddy' in Polish. Mój tatuś was someone I dearly loved, but he was a hands-off dad, somewhat aloof, who let my mom handle all "kid interventions." She would then keep him updated about what was going on. He died much too young at age 63, so I did not get to know him well nor did I have an adult relationship with him. But after having some of the letters from his family translated as well as those my mom wrote to him, I have a deeper understanding of the man who was my father. He was adventurous on the one hand but cautious on the other. Taking risks was not his common practice. He loved his wife and children, but they did not fulfill him. He was a conundrum. I think he was a dreamer.

Chapter 34

The Next Generation

By late summer of 1947, my dad's family learned that my parents were expecting a child. My grandmother had a dream which she wrote about of seeing a blue blanket and my mother holding a baby. Needless to say, they were ecstatic with the idea of new life in the family, a real hope for the future.

Life often gives us bitter pills to swallow, and bad things happen to good people. In my mother's case, she had already swallowed her share of bitter pills. The blue blanket of my grandmother's dream was not to be, because the little girl born in March 1948 only lived for two days. They named her Teresa, and they buried her in an unmarked grave in the children's section of a cemetery in Winchester, England. I find it hard to conceive the extent of my mother's sorrow and pain, especially with the tragedies she experienced in her early life. She was only twenty-eight years old. While growing up, I learned that I could have had an older sister had she lived, while the only thing my mother ever said about the whole matter was that Teresa had only lived two days and mom was unable to carry a baby to full term. I never knew what the medical complications were that caused my sister's death. I had the good fortune to visit the United Kingdom in the 1990s and traveled through Winchester, the Hiltingbury area where my parents had lived, and saw the hospital where I was born. I made a point of trying to find the children's section of the cemetery in Winchester, but since it was an unmarked grave and so many years had passed, it was impossible to identify the site. I think it made my mother happy to know that I was there and tried to find the grave.

Another memory I have about mom's dark time involved white lilacs. Lilacs are one of my all-time favorite flowers of spring. If not the real flower, a fragrance from a lilac-scented candle will do to remind me of the flower I love. When walking past a lilac bush, I must go up to it and smell the flower. I don't think I ever experienced smelling a white lilac, or recall seeing them because mom could not have them in the house. On the day Teresa (or *Terenia* her name in Polish) was born, my dad brought white lilacs to the hospital for mom. Remembering the day she died was forever too raw, so mom could never bear the sight of white lilacs again. Also, since mom would never talk about her firstborn, I never even knew the anniversary of Teresa's death. When that day came around one year, as a kid, I found out the hard way. It was one of those days when I was causing trouble at home, apparently doing something wrong, or whining about this or that. It was a day in late March and my mother's fuse was especially short. She burst into tears after I asked why she was so upset with me, and she said, "Today was the day Terenia died." I don't remember that day being commemorated in any way or talked about again, at least not in front of me.

Both families in Poland were devastated to learn the news that their first grandchild had failed to thrive. All the while, both sides of the family wanted the young couple to return to Poland. As with generations before them, it was the practice that families all stayed together; quite often even lived together. But the war damaged that concept, especially since so many families were torn apart in the aftermath. In Poland, dad's family visited mom's and brought the news of the baby to them in person. Everyone cried. Mom's uncle Franek was there and made it known that he had been saving his money to help mom and dad resettle in Poland. Previously, he had told mom that he had the papers documenting the ownership of her childhood home in Kosów, which could be used for reclamation purposes. It would not bring her any money but it would get them an apartment in one of the resettlement areas. They all wanted my parents to return to their homeland, but my dad had set his sights on leaving England and it was not to live in Poland.

After the loss of Terenia, my mom insisted on having a healthy baby as soon as she could because she desperately wanted to have children, to have a family. She could not delay another pregnancy for fear a different doctor would not realize her medical issues. As a result, mom got pregnant again in September 1948. Everyone was on pins and needles about her pregnancy, with letters back and forth wondering about mom's health and doling out advice. Mom, most of all, was living in a hell because of the tremendous fear of losing a second child, which brought on depression. My grandmother was especially comforting with her loving letters of support. "Have faith in God that all will finally turn out well for you," she wrote.

On May 22, 1949, my mother delivered a healthy baby boy—my brother Andrew was born a month before full term. The proud grandparents, upon seeing photos of the precious new baby boy Serbinski, commented that he looked like royalty. And needless to say, my proud grandfather was very excited because the Serbinski name would live on and he now had a good reason to celebrate. After all, he had gone to church every day for a month before the birth to pray for the safe delivery of a baby boy. After the birth, grandfather took walks through a park in town and looked at all the babies strolling in their carriages, but no child was as stately looking as his new grandson!

My mother always dreamed of having two children, so she insisted on getting pregnant again after my brother Andrew was born. She did so when he was not yet a year old. My parents faced the reality that they were going to be packing up and moving out of the country, so again, it was important to have the same local doctor entrusted with labor and delivery. My mother often said that because she was an only child, she missed having a sibling to share life experiences with, and therefore, desperately wanted two children. Because of this master plan, I believe I would not be on this earth today had mom's firstborn lived. It is documented in their letters to one another during the war that they wanted to have their girl and boy, two children named Teresa and Andrew, the names they had chosen. They lost their firstborn, a girl, and then had their boy. So when I came along, they had their two children, just in a different order, a boy and then a girl. My mother delivered a healthy baby girl in November 1950, and they named her Barbara.

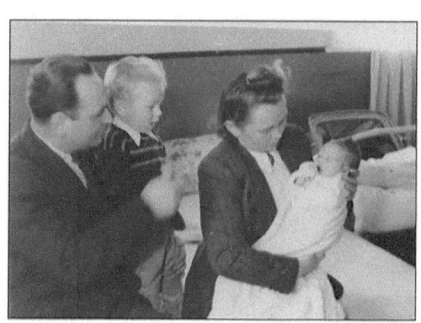

Baby Barbara

Healthy additions to the family, Andrew and Barbara.

3 Growing Up Polish

Chapter 35

Another New Land

By the spring of 1951, it was off to the United States of America. Dad's family all expressed sadness and worry. "What will you do for work?" my grandfather asked. "You will probably need to do manual labor," he went on to say.

Dad's family after the war.

There was so much poverty and destruction everywhere in Europe that my dad felt the United States made more sense and by moving there, they would have more opportunities. Mom and dad took a leap of faith with two babies and set sail to the United States on the S.S America Ocean liner in May 1951.

We came to live in a town along the Ohio River from Pittsburgh in Western Pennsylvania called Ambridge. This was close to where my mother's uncle had settled only months before. The uncle that was my parents' sponsor was the brother of Uncle Franek, mom's priest uncle, and her mother Magdalena. On arrival, the family was penniless, as all their resources were spent on the ocean passage and then for the trip from New York City to the Pittsburgh area. There was no apartment or job waiting. Ambridge was a steel mill town; full of second and third-generation Poles, Hungarians, and others of Eastern European ancestry. A Polish gentleman who owned a rental property, a tiny apartment, let our family stay for free until we were able to get on our feet. American Bridge Steel Company, the steel mill in town, was hiring and my dad got a job.

The idea of a prosperous life and accomplishing the American Dream was always elusive for my parents, even though they raised two children to believe we could reach for the stars and accomplish anything we wanted. "There is nothing you cannot do if you set your mind to do it," my mother would say. Because my parents wanted a family so much, my brother and I personified what made the world go around for them. It was as though their lives were no longer important. What was important was that we become well-educated, successful, and prosperous.

We did not live in Ambridge for very long because it was an industrial town, unlike the green hills and trees of their native Polish region. They quickly found housing, a second-floor walk-up, in the neighboring town of Sewickley, which was a quaint and quiet pedestrian village, an ideal town where they would raise their children. Moving from one flat to another, they eventually were able to save enough money to buy their first and only house. As mom aged, she vowed never to leave the ideal location of her home in this town, because she could walk everywhere: to church, the grocer, the bank, the dry cleaner, and to many different restaurants.

Sewickley was not an ethnic community. We left that behind in Ambridge, with its ethnic meat markets having sawdust on the floor and weird odors, and the Polish Catholic Church where the priests said many masses in the Polish language. On Easter, we would still go to that church to have our eggs blessed on Holy Saturday. The church would be filled with people carrying large baskets full of food which filled the church with aromas of kielbasa, ham, and hard-boiled eggs, all waiting to be blessed for the Easter Sunday breakfast spread. We, on the other hand, carried a tiny basket of painted hardboiled eggs and one simple white egg. This goes back to mom's tradition from Poland where only the eggs were blessed, and most importantly, the lone unpainted white one. In our family, the white hardboiled egg was peeled and cut into four pieces, one for each of us to share with one another on Easter Sunday morning at the breakfast table. This custom is similar to sharing the wafer at Christmas Eve dinner. Sharing the egg is said to bring blessings to each in the family for the coming year.

Sewickley, unlike Ambridge, was more "apple pie and Chevrolet." Early on, while living in Sewickley, I remember my mother referring to us as "DPs." We were unlike the others who lived in the cute little affluent town along the Ohio River. Sewickley had a specialty grocery store, in addition to the A&P, as well as a specialty fish market. It was normal too with a Murphy's five and ten-cent store and a movie theatre where you could see movies all afternoon for twenty-five cents and devour popcorn for fifteen cents. But if you went down to the five and ten-cent store, you could buy popcorn for a dime and the employees allowed you to bring it into the movie theater. As a kid in the winter, I would take the bus alone from our apartment with my ice skates to skate on a pond north of town. This was indeed the perfect all-American town in which to grow up! So, what was the problem? My mom would say our neighbors and others who lived in the village looked down on us for being DPs. "What on earth is a DP?" I wondered. I was told we were Displaced People, people who are refugees who no longer had a country.

We spoke Polish in the home, and no one did that in Sewickley. We ate interesting food; some might call it strange, unlike the food eaten by our neighbors. One of the best menu items in addition to pierogis is *zimne nogi*, literally translated as "cold feet." The feet are pork hocks. Some Poles call it *studzienina*. This dish is served cold and is made of pork broth turned to aspic with pieces of pork knuckle meat, a lot of garlic, and carrots. It's drizzled with white vinegar and eaten with a slice of pumpernickel bread. To this day, I love this dish! We also ate a lot of bigos, which is cooked cabbage with pork and kielbasa. There was also kasza and kiśka. Kasza is groats, a grain like barley only more bitter and kiśka is blood sausage, which is made from some by-products stuffed into sausage skins. This I will never miss eating. So, yes, these could have been considered strange foods!

Our family kept to ourselves, especially my parents. Being a DP meant you were in essence a person without a country, someone forced to leave his native land because of political circumstances. The reference was used as a derogatory term when referring to immigrants, especially those coming from Eastern Europe at that time. In many communities, DPs associate with other DPs. Some immigrants who came earlier in history, the old immigrant families, didn't care for the new DPs immigrating because they were the poor, the wretched outcasts left over from the war. This feeling of not belonging may have been subjective, but prevalent nonetheless.

DP camps were set up all over Europe after the war to temporarily house those refugees from Eastern Europe, those who were former inmates of Nazi German concentration camps, those who no longer had a village to return to, or those who found that returning to their homeland would endanger their lives. Two years post World War II, about 850,000 people still lived in DP camps across Europe, which was populated by Poles, Latvians, Russians, Czechoslovaks, Armenians, Yugoslavs, Greeks, Ukrainians, Lithuanians, and Jews. We were the lucky ones to be a part of the

Polish Army forces, because my parents were demobilized in the United Kingdom from our existence as a family in the Resettlement program from a Polish refugee camp in Great Britain. This was how we were able to travel to the United States in search of a better life, but relying on the help of others.

Not much has changed over the years. In times of unrest and war in today's global society, neighboring nations open their borders to refugees for humanitarian reasons. This we have seen all over the Middle East and Northern Africa in our contemporary history. Presently in our society, both in our country and around the globe, there is anti-immigrant/refugee rhetoric making it very difficult for people without a country to start over. It's never been easy for refugees to integrate into a new society, and historical countries, both culturally and politically. Often, members of a Diaspora[31] express thoughts of returning to their native country, which prevents them from fully integrating into the host country. It has been said that most people don't choose to leave their country unless they are forced to do so. In the process of leaving their native country, they hunger to start a new life, while some, if they could are eager to go back to the old country.

I saw this attitude toward integration in my parents. Even though they were not active in any Polish societies or organizations, they in their own way made it known that Poland was their home country and their hearts were still there. In my opinion, my parents became reluctant United States citizens. They did not obtain their U.S. citizenship for the sheer love of country, as I would expect, but because they had to since they were a part of the refugee resettlement program. This gave them a path to citizenship. In my naiveté, I was never able to understand this apprehensive attitude. I was American, regardless of whether we spoke a different language at home or not, and I could not understand why anyone would not embrace the language of their new country to learn it properly and to integrate into a nation that was founded on freedom and justice.

---

[31] Diaspora is a term that refers to a scattering or migration of people who are forcibly displaced from their ancestral lands to another nation.

My mother spoke English much better than my dad who did not have much interest in learning it well. These observations only surfaced as I became older.

Looking back on how my father did not want to embrace his new land, I felt he missed opportunities to have a better life in the United States. Not ever walking in my parents' shoes nevertheless gave me the unfounded license to criticize. Mom often said they did the best they could within their circumstances. I do believe there was an element of sorrow and regret in my dad's heart, maybe about the life choices he made, which kept him from fully assimilating into American society. I believe that is why he did not learn the English language well and did not want to socialize. In his mind, he was from somewhere foreign and since he couldn't go back in time to be happy, this venture in a new country with a family became a cross to bear.

I am proud to know that my mother, after fifty years of living in the United States, did write, "I am proud to live in the United States where no one would bang on my door in the middle of the night to arrest me and take me off to prison." At the same time, she was critical of a country that would invade another and call it just, referring to the 2003 United States invasion of Iraq. As she said, "Invading another country can never be a just cause."

As much as I understood this reasoning about the Iraqi invasion, I was never able to embrace such a statement, since my son, her grandson, was in the Marine Corps and did three tours in Iraq following the invasion. In retrospect, she was absolutely correct in her assessment of the whole Iraq invasion debacle. Fortunately, for me and my family, we were blessed. My son Christopher made it through to discharge, alive and well.

Chapter 36

Making Our Way in the United States

Polish was my first language because I learned English by going to school. One of my first memories of school was being in a Christmas pageant in kindergarten, reciting a poem in Polish, with my mother standing in the wings giving me prompts in case I forgot a line. As with all kids, I wanted to fit in, but sometimes, that was difficult. I did not really feel that I was the same as other kids. It may have been easier to live in an ethnically Polish community where everyone spoke the language, ate the same food, and had similar struggles. In our situation, the next best thing was having another family around that was Polish. My parents developed a beautiful friendship with a couple who came to our flat one day and invited my parents to join a Polish organization, a White Eagle Club in the City of Pittsburgh. My parents went a couple of times, but socializing with people was not what my dad liked to do. That couple who extended a hand of friendship to my parents became their best friends. The four of them would socialize at our apartment or we would travel to see them in their home in Pittsburgh.

My fondest recollection of those early years was when they played bridge together until all hours of the night, and then when conversations and often arguments would erupt, I was within earshot. Those conversations were not always about the card game, which is what fascinated me. They would each talk of the war and their experiences. Kaz and Jola's experiences were very different from those of my parents because of where they grew up in Poland. Jola was from Warsaw and Kaz was from somewhere in the west. Kaz, short for Kazimierz, spent time in a German POW camp in France and had opinions about the French and the Jews. He died very young so I don't know much about what he went through, nor did I ever ask. Jola on the other hand lived a long life and was a dear friend to my mom. She had been involved in the Warsaw Uprising in 1944 and grew up in the Polish capital city ready to defend it when the time came. She spoke of having a fairly normal life in occupied Warsaw during the early years of the war, telling of going to school, dances, and out on dates. All that changed once the Rising began. Her real name was actually Lydia. The underground gave her the name of Jola, which stuck with her until the day she died. After she survived the destruction and surrender of Warsaw, she was sent to a German POW camp until the end of the war. She and Kaz met and married in England after the war and also never returned to Poland to live, but they would go back often to visit family.

Late at night, the four bridge-playing friends would debate global events, current and past, as well as argue about what went wrong with the bridge hands. As a young child, I did not understand all the global issues, but what stayed with me and impressed me the most was their passion for past and current affairs and global politics. Supporting each other in a new land was what brought them together; their love for Poland was what bound them together for the rest of their lives.

Having our family separated by such distance and news of family members dying were tragic for my mom. Dear Uncle Franek died in March 1961. This saddened my mother tremendously, but I don't remember being told of it when it actually happened. I knew he had died but only learned of the circumstances through the actual letter that mom received, which I had translated. Mom received it from Franek's priest friend and caretaker, who outlined his last days. Apparently, he had been gravely ill with a heart condition. His last mass was celebrated the month before his death and lasted an hour and a half because Franek could not stand at the altar very long at any one time. In a return letter, mom had asked his caretaker if any of her belonging were found among his. There were a few items left from the Kosów house. Franek had them shipped to his new resettlement location but they somehow disappeared. The only items left in his possession were some family vital certificates and estate documents which the caretaker said he would send along with some photographs. The letter went onto say that the last few years of his life were full of suffering and sadness. He usually spent a month at a time in the hospital because of his recurring illness. His failing health was a source of depression which was why he did not talk about it in letters to his niece. The serious nature of his decline had to be a shock to mom.

Two years later in 1963, dad's father Marcin died, and then his mother Paulina passed away nine years later. What started out as a very small family torn apart by war was shrinking.

Chapter 37

Poland on the World Stage

When it came to global news and issues, my parents were passionate and serious. In the evening when the nightly news was on, no one dared to talk or ask a question for fear that some nugget of information would be missed. My parents took their politics and social issues very seriously, especially since that time in history, the 1950s and 1960s, was consumed by their country's arch-nemesis, the Soviet Union. Mom often spoke about how misrepresented and misunderstood the people of Poland were following the end of the war. Much of this comes from how the Soviets treated the Poles. Stalin was the enemy for the first two years of the war but after Hitler invaded the Soviet Union, Stalin became a powerful Western ally during the years that followed. Therefore, any alleged or factual maltreatment of the Poles was suppressed. It was more or less brushed under the rug by the West which looked the other way. While Poland was under communist rule, the people of Poland were told they should fear speaking about any abuse or suffering under the Soviet siege. Those Poles who fled to the West either found the topic too painful to remember, or they feared for their families back home enough not to write or speak about it. Therefore, history did not speak to the facts of the Soviet's involvement in war atrocities until the fall of communism in Eastern Europe in 1990.

Since that time, survivors and their families are playing catchup, trying to chronicle what happened to their soldiers, relatives, and civilian family members, trying to make sure that this time, facts are properly documented. I remember how upset my mother would become when certain movies or books came out about the Holocaust and how Poles were left out of the dialogue since only the Jews were victimized. The world had a tendency to portray the Jews as the only victims of World War II. She would tell me about all the Polish university professors, police officers, government officials, and priests who were sent to Nazi extermination camps and how many Poles were arrested and killed for hiding and helping Jews during the war. A well-known victim of Nazi abuse was a priest, who volunteered to take the place of a man selected for death, a Jew, for an infraction committed at Auschwitz. For his selfless act, that priest, the Polish Franciscan Maximillian Kolbe, has since been canonized a saint in the Catholic Church. There is no doubt that there were Poles who also persecuted the Jews, but the other side, the side of kindness and justice, does not get the same publicity.

For over seventy years, the Jewish people have protected their history to make sure that society never forgets what happened to their people at the hand of Hitler and the Nazi regime both before and during the war. The Poles not only fell victim to the atrocities of Nazi Germany, but also to those of Stalin's Soviet Union. Together, the Nazis and Soviets killed six million Polish citizens during World War II. Of those six million, three million were Polish Christians. Three million were Polish Jews. It is only recently that much is being written and documented about that time in history.

In the decade before the war, Poland had the largest Jewish population of any one European country, which made Poland the perfect location for the majority of the Nazi extermination camps. The country was ravaged by the destruction that took place on its land against its people; the country was scarred by the hatred that took place in the extermination camps within its borders. The country was then raped by the ideological forces of a communist government taking over the creative and free minds of its people which lasted for five decades. Yet, there are continuous media references that refer to the World War II death camps as Polish extermination camps, instead of Nazi death camps. The Polish people suffered their own Holocaust, their genocide during the war by two aggressors, and could not speak of it. The Red Army liberated all of Poland by design, which laid a path for Stalin's claim to the whole of Poland, creating it as a communist satellite country in 1946. The Soviet atrocities lay dormant for years. It has taken the past twenty years to reveal to the world how many were murdered in Katyń, how many died from deportation, and why so many Poles, men, women, and children, were displaced all over the world. The Nazis had their Nuremberg Trials, which were judged as crimes against humanity, enslavement, or deportation of civilians. These crimes were based on persecution, on political, religious, and racial grounds. There was no opportunity for such an accounting against the Soviets who committed atrocities and war crimes, or for the Polish people to face their villain in a court. It is necessary to set the record straight as to what happened because the Polish nation was manipulated during and after the war by the West, to Stalin's satisfaction.

That culture is what angered mom, the outward defiling of the country she loved. This disrespect of Poles over the years infuriated her, as well as knowing what Joseph Stalin and his successors were able to orchestrate—a veil of communist secrecy. That veil of secrecy was very difficult for my mother and other justice-seeking Poles to understand and accept. It prevailed throughout the Cold War and was not lifted until communism fell in Eastern Europe and throughout the former Soviet Union.

Mom was at least able to share some of her story with her family and others who expressed interest, but all those very real haunting memories went to the grave with her as they did with so many other survivors. Since the fall of communism, some of these stories have come out of hiding and continue to do so. The fact that the Russian government has slowly allowed access to archived documents implicating their former government in those vile acts toward the Poles has helped to excavate deeply buried memories from many people after more than seventy years.

Chapter 38

Living with Trauma

As life goes on, we cannot predict how the negative experiences from a person's past will continue to define, haunt, and sometimes ruin that person's future. My sweet and loving dad lived through trauma while defending his country in September 1939, then experienced harsh and difficult conditions in Lithuania and then in a Soviet prison and later fought on the battlefields of Italy. He was a very private person, so he was either not able to share his private experiences or chose not to. For these reasons and those unknown, his personality changed into that of a "loner." Perhaps, he took after his mother who was unlike his social father, but the early stories of my dad as a young adult portrayed him as a social being, having many school friends and army buddies.

All I know is that he felt unfulfilled in his life, as he blamed the war for interfering with a prosperous future. He remained a steelworker all of his short post-war adult life, and ended that career as a welder, which is an honorable line of work; but skilled labor was not his vision of a life-long career. Before the war, he was a professional, working for an insurance company in his hometown. He attended law school for two years and was with the Army reserve in the officer cadet program. Corporate law or insurance law would have paved the way for that prosperous future. In retrospect, I see a man who tried to find some of his dignity by drinking and dreaming of a better life for himself and his family. I see the hardships of dad doing manual labor for low pay which resulted in his developing and suffering from health issues. I think he tried to make the best of the life he had, but in his mind, it was not enough when he ached for the country that raised him. Reasons remained as to why he did not go back to the hometown he longed for, which included financial concerns. But also, his town was now in a foreign country and his family lived elsewhere. There was also the fear of re-arrest. He longed for the past, not his present-day Poland. Understanding now that he was always fighting his demons puts things into perspective. I remember a few Christmas Eve dinners when I was young, dad would have a few glasses of wine, and we would listen to a Polish radio station and to Polish Christmas carols. He would start to become nostalgic, then emotional, and then would begin to cry. The past is a very powerful reminder of one's successes and failures, of loves lost and found, of what happened and what might have been. It was not enough for my dad to celebrate the family's present. He grieved for his past.

My mother did talk more about and documented more of her war experiences. In hindsight, her behavior is easier to understand knowing the depth of her losses. She wrote of her puzzling encounters with the past and how they affected her. She wrote an essay called *"The Fraud That I am or Too Many Monkeys on My Back."* She considered herself a fraud because her outward persona was one of confidence, reasonable behavior, and self-sufficiency, which she mastered especially after my dad passed away. But out of nowhere, the deep-rooted fears of her past would take over involuntarily in different situations. Because she considered herself a no-nonsense type of person, she asked, "Why can't I control my responses when some stimuli make me fearful and bring on panic?" When she wrote the document about her war experiences in the mid-1980s, she said that even fifty years after the traumatic events, she would still wake up in the middle of the night physically exhausted from running and hiding from the Russians in her sleep, sweating, heart racing, and gasping for breath. Little things like spring cleaning would bring on an episode of panic brought on by needing to put something away in a cabinet but not being able to open the door of the cabinet. This simple act would bring on a panic attack. "Not being able to open a door for the sane person," she said, "is nothing. It only takes a bit more time and patience." But to my mom, it would bring on full panic because a door was locked and she could not get in or out. The situation did not even lend itself to the moment, but mom still felt trapped, helpless, and out of control under those circumstances.

I do think that my mom's incessant journaling helped her cope with her pent-up passions and emotions about certain topics, whether they were about her past or whether they were about current political events involving the United States and Europe. This may have been a therapeutic avenue for her to release her suppressed feelings. As Emma contemplated writing her story, she also wrote that "Just remembering those details again was like pieces of me were tearing away from my body," and "the vultures of the past were whirling above my head."

As a result of various memories and triggers, Emma wrote that one day, while she was shopping for groceries, her cart was full and ready for check-out, and without consciously realizing why, she felt her heart racing and she was sweating. She then became aware that someone nearby was speaking Russian. That was enough for panic to set in and irrational thoughts to take over, accompanied by an overwhelming need to flee. She had to fight the urge to abandon the cart in the middle of the store and run out as quickly as she could. In today's world, this type of panicked behavior would be categorized as a classic case of post-traumatic stress disorder or PTSD.

Another one of mom's trauma symptoms appeared when there was a change in her routine. Since my brother and I moved away from Sewickley and after my dad died, mom loved to stay at home and she did not like the idea of traveling. When it came time for her to see my children in Chicago for holidays, the idea of leaving her sanctuary, her home, was very frightening. After all, she was traveling by airplane to my home and she knew she would be safe, but nevertheless, that irrational panic plagued her. Days prior to the departure, she would have sleepless nights, fretting about leaving her house. There were a couple of times when I was to pick her up at the airport and encountered unusual traffic, causing me to be late. Mom would already be in a panic upon my arrival. She did realize that this was the result of the fear she experienced while traveling from prison to prison and to the labor camp in the middle of Asiatic Russia, then to freedom by way of foreign lands. She was "a speck of dust in the middle of nowhere," as she called herself. Even while realizing why she reacted this way, the same sleepless nights and fretting took over whenever she was invited to visit. The panic attacks returned each and every time. Because my mother was such a strong person, I never realized how much she suffered.

My mother's fear of being lost was profound. I remember when I was a little girl, we would take family vacations, or just go for a long ride to the Pennsylvania countryside. The car ride, in dad's pride and joy, the used 1956 Buick, always resulted in our getting lost at some point. Mom and dad would begin to argue about why they got lost, what was the correct road, and then about how they should get back on the right road to find their way. She was the navigator, the one with the map. Panic would set in and she could not make sense of it. They each blamed the other for getting lost. After my dad died and mom was on her own, she drove the only new car they ever bought together, a 1979 Pontiac Sunbird. She would not venture out of her comfort zone around town, only going by car to stores she knew and places that were familiar. When she needed to get out of the house and out of her normal routine, she made sure she went somewhere familiar where she would not get turned around and not know where she was. Therefore, she never took long trips.

My husband Alan would logically try to explain that to visit us in Chicago was easy and all mom had to do was to get to I-79, which was close to her, follow the signs to the Pennsylvania Turnpike, and drive west. A running joke ensued that to go anywhere, "just get on I-79." The logic was there, but there was no way she could do anything of the sort. The traumatic response to this fear ran deep and all those times when we laughed about it, I did not comprehend how severe her fear was. It got worse as she grew older. Even around her town of Sewickley, getting lost became more and more of a problem. Mom would often drive to see her friend Jola, even at night. Several years before her stroke, she set out to see Jola and when it was time to go home, it was dark outside. On her way home, mom became disoriented and found herself on an expressway, heading away from her home instead of toward it. She had been to Jola's house hundreds of times, but after she panicked, I don't know how she got home! The end of the story is that she would never again drive to Jola's house, not even during the day. A few years later, mom had an automobile accident, totaling the Sunbird. She was shaken up emotionally but physically okay. She was forced to replace the Sunbird with a used Chevy Cavalier, but only traveled close to home.

Emma often wondered what her life would have been like had the war not happened. She likened the wondering to a decision of which road to take, as in Robert Frost's poem, *The Road Less Traveled*. Being able to make the choice of which road to take gives you, as she puts it, "decisive control" over your life; when given an order, you are given a set of obstacles to overcome and then need to make the best of it. In her case, mom had to deal with the war, the obstacles which broke down all structures of society in all the countries it touched, the countless families it displaced and destroyed, which also destroyed peoples' personal dreams and ambitions. But Emma lived the advice her parents gave her when she was growing up: "Hope for the best, plan for the worst, and take what comes with humor and style. Only rarely will anything turn out as badly as you feared. Don't waste time imagining the worst." This was the way she viewed life. At the same time, I feel that my mother, even though she had great gusto for life, spent her entire life living with caution, the self-protection needed to guard against those demons that made her feel vulnerable and helpless. Both my parents had similar feelings about being dealt a bad hand of cards in life, but the similarity ends with mom's innate optimism.

My dad was not as philosophical as mom was. He was more pragmatic and simply acted as though the war had ruined his life, without actually saying it.

Tatuś, my dad in Polish, eventually withdrew into a self-imposed and unnatural prison cell of isolation. After being beaten down by life, my dad gave up, gave in to his illnesses, and died a few years after he was diagnosed with atherosclerosis which led to kidney failure. Needing weekly kidney dialysis took a toll on his attitude even more. By then, he had educated his two children, married off his daughter, and was successful in getting on Social Security Disability.

My dad on my wedding day

Tatuś never saw his parents after leaving for war in September of 1939, yet his parents lived for quite a while after the war. He only saw his sister Stasia when she came to the United States the summer before his death in December 1979. I was glad to meet her and I am sure he appreciated that she made the trip; but since I was not living at home at the time, I wonder what they spoke about and how they interacted. Were there any unkind words or a blame game going on? After she left to return home to Poland, I believe he felt like he was "done." He fulfilled all his responsibilities, gave in to the illnesses, and then, he died. His sister was four years older than he, and lived until 1988, dying at the age of seventy-six from cancer. He died at sixty-three.

My mother, in contrast, lived a long and independent life after dad's death. She became social with neighbors and others in town, something I am convinced she would have done earlier had my dad not been such a recluse. Everyone knew Emma in Sewickley and since she loved to take walks around town, she became a known fixture. Mom enjoyed her children and grandchildren and would travel to visit us, despite not wanting to leave her home. She took care of my children a few times when we went out of town, which I now realize had to be difficult for her. Being responsible for her grandchildren while being away from her own home and its perceived safety had to be both physically and emotionally draining for her, but she did it anyway. She always wanted to help and to please. At Christmas time, she was the chief pierogi maker for Christmas Eve dinner. Only after making the required amount of pierogi and uszka (little mushroom filled dumplings for the beet soup), would she enjoy her one and only wine cooler for the holiday celebration.

For Emma, family was more important than anything else. Birthdays were always a treat for my children when they were little. mom would call them and sing *"Happy Birthday"* to them, but her version was "Happy Birsday to U," as she pronounced it. The kids would roll their eyes and giggle that grandma mispronounced the words, yet they expected this show over the phone every year. This memory of their Polish grandma is one of their fondest to this day. She would always dote on them by sending them silly cards and valentines just to send them something in the mail. When it was time to receive presents, she made a big fuss about the smallest thing, be it for her feast day or Christmas. In her mind, the thought behind the gift was more important than the gift itself.

Even though haunted by her past, mom tried never to show it nor give in to it. It angered her when the demons managed to take control. Much has been researched over the last decades about the effects of trauma resulting from witnessing or being subjected to violence, seeing violence during military action, and being abused or enslaved through human trafficking or abused by a spouse. It has taken society much time to understand that people are vulnerable to various types of traumas and need help finding ways to cope. During my mother's adult life, the conversation about her needing professional help because of past trauma never came up. It was not on anyone's radar that she could benefit from treatment. PTSD was never associated with mom's trauma and the subsequent effects. Nor did I realize or understand the depth of her wounds or the extent of her suffering. She knew why there were certain triggers for the cold sweats and the fear of getting lost. Consequently, somehow, she knew she just needed to deal with them. That will to live and fight was so strong that it survived all conflicts, challenges, and hurdles.

It was not until a few years before her death that she slowed down. She knew she was not as spry as when she was younger and decided not to travel because of the physical and emotional toll it took to leave her house. That insurance policy she talked about and the phrase "It's no fun getting old" would come up in conversations more often. Andy and I came to see her more frequently, still taking those walks to the waterfall and around town.

Eventually, we had to take care of her after her stroke. In the hospital immediately following the stroke and once in the nursing home, she told everyone that she had been a nurse during the war. She was very proud of that accomplishment despite her dementia. In the early years when the family moved to Sewickley, she tried to get a nursing job at the hospital, but the hours were in conflict with taking care of two little kids. This is why she turned to work out of the house doing re-weaving, mending, and sewing, which ironically was her early career in Poland, and that of dad's mother.

When hospice nurses told me that she did not have much longer to live, I called and asked Andy and his wife Judy to fly in to say goodbye. During his visit, I also called one of the parish priests to come to the nursing home and administer the last rites of the Catholic Church. Since this particular priest was from Poland,

I knew that having her hear some of the prayers in Polish would make her happy.

My girls, Alan, Andy, his wife Judy, and I gathered in mom's room as we held hands and said the Lord's Prayer. At the end when we all said "Amen," mom opened her eyes, lifted her head, and said "Amen." She then lived for another nine days.

Soon came the time for her to join her mother and father and her husband in heaven. During her time in the nursing home, as her dementia got worse, she often spoke about her mother. Mom often would become frantic thinking that her mother must be worried about her, not knowing where she was and whether she was safe. Mom repeatedly asked me to call her mother, to make sure her mother knew her whereabouts so she would not worry. I always promised I would contact her.

This I found very interesting and wondered why she was so concerned about her mother, the stern parent of her childhood. But in reality, it was not that puzzling as I thought about it. Since mom's personality was one that wanted to please and help, it's not surprising that she always sought her mother's approval. During the war, her mother had to have experienced frantic times not knowing where her daughter was or even if her daughter was alive. And during those times in the nursing home, the past came forward, mom needed to make sure her mother knew she was safe. It all makes sense now. Her mother always insisted her daughter be raised to be tough on the outside yet have a soft heart. This strength of character was what made mom a successful mother, grandmother, partner, and friend.

She must have been at peace with her dad because in that stage of dementia, she never spoke of him but she did talk about and dreamed of her husband, my dad. Mom would recount how he would come to visit her in her nursing home room at night in a dream. Very often, she would say it was "time to go and see Tatuś." Mom always referred to her husband as Tatuś.

Emma did have a very full life—full of adventure, intrigue, suffering, trauma, love, and laughter. The majority of it was somewhat routine, living in a peaceful little town in the United

States. Sewickley was similar to the town of her youth in Poland. The obvious difference was that her life in the United States took place within the boundaries of her small family: two children and a husband (albeit for a short time) and eventually five grandchildren, and a daughter-in-law. My son came home with his fiancée the month before she died, allowing him a chance to see his grandmother for what might be the last time, to say goodbye. She held his hand and spoke to him passionately and seriously about something, as she often did. As a result, he cried. Later, he said he didn't know the point of what she said, but seeing her like that, loving her, and knowing he would probably not see her again, made him cry. They had a special bond.

On the last two days of her life, I spent many hours talking to her, mainly thanking her for being such a wonderful mother who taught by example. She taught me that family comes first, above all else. She taught me to be a patient mother. She taught me always to do the right thing. She taught me the meaning of love. I felt she needed to know that it was okay with me for her to go on, to be with her mother, father, and husband. I told her that I would be okay and that my family would be okay. I told her that Andy had his wife and their family would all be okay. She was free to go. On the afternoon of the day she died, there was a severe thunderstorm with tornado warnings in the area. The threat was so severe that it is her residence's policy to move all patients into the hallways as a precaution against windows being blown into the rooms. All bedridden patients had their beds moved into the hall. I was able to sit with her in the hallway and hold her hand, even as awkward as it was with all the hustle and bustle in the area as she was dying. It was good to be there with her to give her some comfort.

The storm blew over and hospice nurses came to give her a sponge bath and to make her comfortable. I told her I would come back in the evening. There was a time before her stroke that mom would ask me whether I had any regrets or reservations about how I was raised. She must have been reflective then about her life and the choices that she and my dad made which affected me as I was growing up. I found the question both puzzling and awkward to answer. When I answered that I had no regrets, she immediately said defensively that they did what they could with what they had and they only had the best intentions in mind. There was no "dress rehearsal" for parenting, she would say.

In my last thank you, I assured her that she was a wonderful mother and that I always felt loved. I thanked her for all the sacrifices she made for me. Later that evening, she died in her sleep before I was able to return. Mom died on June 19, 2009, which was Alan's and my wedding anniversary. She died two years and four months after her stroke.

She was and continues to be my inspiration, and I miss her every day.

4 My Adult Polish Life - Without Mom

Epilogue

In the fall of 2013, I connected with a Polish second cousin with whom mom corresponded after all of her first cousins had passed away. When I started this project, I knew of this cousin, but possibly other relatives might still be alive and living in Poland. I decided to write letters to relatives who might be out there. Because mom kept so many random papers, coupons, and letters on her desk, I found a few old envelopes with return addresses affixed to them. Four letters went out to various addresses and as fate would have it, one of the relatives contacted me via email. She wondered why my mom stopped writing and thought that maybe she had gotten sick or had passed away. I was thrilled to get any response, especially since this cousin, Ewa, had moved and the address I used was an old one. A former neighbor of Ewa's had seen the letter, knew where the family had moved, and hand-delivered it. This was serendipitous. Ewa is my second cousin; her grandfather and mine, Marcin, were brothers.

After exchanging emails and connecting through Skype, I realized that Ewa would never travel to the United States to see me, so I would need to go to Poland to see her. I suggested that I travel to see them and also to visit my mom's hometown of Kosów which is still in Ukraine, as well as my need to visit Warsaw. As it turned out, Ewa said that she and her family traveled to Kosów periodically to visit some of her family on her mother's side and that she would be pleased to take me to Ukraine when I came.

I set out for Poland by myself to meet these people I had never met. I had to laugh at how easily I embraced the idea of going to meet total strangers, as in my wildest imagination, they could well be serial killers! And they invited me to stay in their home, not knowing me. What if I was the serial killer! But they welcomed me into their home without reservation. To my delight, I was able to experience and learn from them about current Polish culture, learn about their lives and experiences under communism, hear and speak the language, and also experience firsthand Ukrainian people and their culture. Since Ewa and her family spoke no English, the onus was on me to speak Polish exclusively. My language skills had greatly diminished over the years since leaving my family home and no longer having my mother alive to keep the language alive. The strain of having to express my thoughts and respond to their question made the trip exhausting. After two weeks, I was ready to come home. Describing my situation to my brother, I thought my language skills, including vocabulary and grammar, were at least at the second-grade level before I left, but after returning, I realized they were actually at a two-year-old's level! There is a lot of truth to the saying that "If you don't use it, you lose it"!

I learned that my grandfather Marcin was the only one who perished during the war. Another of his brothers, about whom mom never spoke, Kazimierz, who was in the Polish border patrol before the war, was arrested by the Soviets and sent to Siberia. He survived and was released returning to Poland in the mid-1950s, only to die a few years later after choking on a piece of bread. This I learned from Ewa. Mom spoke of Ewa often probably because she was my age. Andy actually met her and her husband Jacek when he traveled to Poland in the early 1970s. My mother was so delighted that he traveled to Poland and was able to meet her family while some aunts, uncles, and cousins were still alive. He also met Stasia, dad's sister.

My greatest satisfaction from the visit to Kosów was finding my mother's childhood home. Because I took with me old photos of her house from before and after the war, I was able to identify the property perfectly once we came upon it. I even had the address of the property, ul. Smodniawska 254. Initially, we could not find it. We were able to solicit help from a Polish gentleman who had lived in the area for decades and he said he remembered mom's family. The situation was opportune. The address of the property had changed, but the man gave perfect directions, and there it was. The pre-war photo of mom on the second-floor balcony of her home, staring out onto the horizon, looking so peaceful and content, is priceless.

Mom's childhood home with me in front in 2013

Mom's cousin Ada in front of mom's house 1956

Mom on her then balcony in the 1930's

Then the opportunity to see the house as it looks today and imagine my mom on that balcony was equally exciting. However, finding the house, as much as it meant to me, seemed a bit hollow and surreal both at the time and later upon reflection. I realized that it should have been mom who went back to find her house, not me. The pain I felt and even remember to this day is the pain of thinking about her past and the circumstances which led to her leaving her home and her family, never to return. Those circumstances can never be changed.

The house is only a physical structure. What it does represent are mom's memories that I could not recreate with my visit. Finding the house does help me to establish a connection to mom and her past, her town, and her history. This gave me quiet comfort. For many years, mom felt sad when thinking of her town, but she had those memories and photos of living in Kosów as a young child and young woman. The reason she gave for not returning to Poland later in life was that she feared re-arrest, and she had no immediate family there to visit, but I'm sure it was also because the town was no longer in Poland. Her fear of re-arrest was more significant than she admitted and it was probably better for her to have those memories which would never change. Re-entering a town that was now in a foreign country could have altered those memories. The best gift I received as a result of exploring my family's past and traveling to Poland was developing a relationship with my cousin, her husband, their daughter Ania, and her son Tymek. Both Ania and Ewa had collected family information and many photographs to share with me. They had started a family tree. Ewa shared a couple of photographs which included the unknown brother Kazimierz and photos of my mom as a small child which I had never seen. This "walk down memory lane" with my family was a precious gift.

Having family, even though they are distant relatives by lineage and by geography, is still a wonderful feeling. While in Kosów, we took much time visiting the two cemeteries in town. The one close to my mom's childhood home, the Catholic cemetery, was filled with very old tombstones and I found names of mom's relatives who had died when she lived there, such as her great grandmother and some great uncles. What I found the most rewarding was seeing two common graves clearly marked as a memorial and final resting place for those murdered by Ukrainian Nationalists on the two dates in March and those who died in April 1944. On one of those dates was the murder of my grandmother, Magdalena, and I had found her final resting place.

In retrospect, the trip to Kosów, Ukraine brings home the idea that history does repeat itself. The area that I visited was a piece of the former independent Poland that was taken over by Stalin during the first two years of the war. It was incorporated into Ukrainian SSR in the Soviet Union. A mere few weeks after my visit, the now Independent Republic of Ukraine, established after the fall of Communism in 1990, was fighting off its former master, Russia, who eventually annexed some of Eastern Ukraine back into the Russian fold, the Crimean Peninsula. Some may say that Vladamir Putin, a former KGB agent, fashions himself as the twenty-first century Stalin, striving for the glory days of the Soviet Union with its powers of intimidation. Kosów is in the western part of Ukraine and has not been touched by the hostilities, but economically, it has felt the pain and its people live in fear of the war with Russia spreading to their area.

The saddest observation of the Ukraine that I witnessed is how economically deprived it has become. The country is under siege politically and economically, leaving the people with an uncertain future, because it never got on its feet following the end of communism. Adding to the economic problems is the fact that because of political strife, the country's resources have been drained. Fighting in the Eastern region, has been going on now for over four years. This conflict is still being experienced between the Russian-backed separatists and Ukrainian government loyalists. In my opinion, the people of Kosów live in a third-world country economically with much unemployment, crumbling infrastructure, and without a prospect for a better future, especially for their young adults. Ewa's nephew is married, has a baby son, lives with his mother, and has no job.

The fighting in Eastern Ukraine began in November 2013 and then the following March, Russia annexed Crimea. Putin said this was necessary because he wanted to protect all the Russian-speaking people in the region. This was Hitler's reasoning for taking over the central European lands in 1938-39, to protect the ethnic Germans. It was also Stalin's reasoning for invading Poland's Kresy. History continues to repeat itself.

At greatest risk are the civilian Ukrainians still living in the battleground hotspots of the Eastern part of the country. People there have little food, except for what they can grow on their small patches of land which are peppered with shrapnel. Their daily lives are lived in a war zone where civilians are still being killed. The country has been devastated, raped by what Moscow through the separatists wants to accomplish, which is to take back the eastern region of Ukraine and return it to Mother Russia.

When I walked the streets of Kosów, I thought that I was looking not just at a third-world nation by today's standards, but a nineteenth-century village during a time even before my mother's birth. The obvious visual differences are that today, the roads have automobiles and there are satellite dishes on some of the buildings, and many people use cell phones. The town looks very old and has peddlers on every block selling mushrooms, garlic, bread, and herbs and hungry, scavenging dogs roaming everywhere.

Kosów 2013

Streets of Kosów in 2013.

At the hostel where we stayed, there were photos on the wall in the upstairs hallway depicting Kosów in a better time although these photos were not dated. There was a photograph of a huge swimming pool in town, which had to have been one of the focal points of summer life for years, full of people enjoying the summer weather. We drove past the actual site of the pool and saw it abandoned and full of weeds. Other photos showed a vibrant business district, while today, the streets are full of poverty-stricken peddlers. On the trip to Kosów, I witnessed many horse-drawn carts with men and women walking their cows in the middle of the road for their afternoon exercise. Seemingly not much has changed over the decades. While driving to the town, we noticed how bad the roads were as we dodged enormous potholes by weaving around them, for fear of a flat tire. On the return trip, we lost a hub cap and eventually did get a flat tire. I might add that while we waited forever to cross the border through the checkpoint to re-enter Poland, our car stalled and we had to push it across the border.

During that trip, I had the good fortune to be in Poland during All Saints Day and All Souls Day. All Saints Day is not just a Catholic Holy Day of Obligation but also a national holiday all over Poland. If All Saints Day occurs on a weekday, schools and businesses are closed. Poles honor and celebrate their dearly departed, tending to their graves and flooding the cemeteries to do so. I have never seen so many people visiting gravesites before. We visited several cemeteries in three towns. For the local people, it is actually a social occasion where they meet up with friends they have not seen in a while and exchange pleasantries. Ewa and Ania made wreaths and brought candles and flowers to freshen the gravesites of family members. Just outside the cemeteries, people sell replacement candles and real or plastic flowers. This is a thriving ancillary business surrounding this occasion. Ewa even brought a broom and cleaning products to clean a couple of the tombstones which were neglected over the previous year. I was fortunate to see the graves of my mom's three favorite cousins: Ewa's father Franciszek, and his two sisters Ada and Luśia.

We then traveled to Gliwice where my dad's family had resettled. I had a map of the huge cemetery where my grandparents and aunt are interred. I found my grandmother's gravesite which also housed my aunt's grave, but we could not find my grandfather's site. Ewa told me that if no one takes care of a gravesite and/or does not pay the cemetery yearly for its general upkeep, the gravesite will no longer be there. I purchased some candles and flowers to put on my aunt's and grandmother's stone. But to my surprise, it was in immaculate condition. I wondered whom I should thank for the upkeep. My aunt died in 1988, so who has been paying for the grave all these years? Having relatives can bring both joy and sadness into family lives. For me, having only one brother while growing up and no aunts or uncles or grandparents close by, family life was simple. When friends comment about family arguments that escalate to the point where members don't speak to other members, or when something happens and nobody really knows what or why, the result is the same; they stop speaking to one another. To this, I cannot relate.

After reading some of my mom's letters, I learned that there were other distant relatives on both sides of the family that I did not know about. My mom tried her best to communicate with as many relatives as were alive, but shared little about them with me. She was the chief communications officer in the family, which included writing to my dad's parents and sister. When she spoke of the past in general terms, not wanting to share any detailed information, she would say, "Dawno i nie prawda." "So long ago and no longer true" is the literal translation.

Conferences

I had the good fortune to take another trip to Poland the following year in September 2014 to attend a conference in Warsaw which was held by the Kresy-Siberia Foundation, an online foundation and virtual museum. The museum memorializes the human stories and losses surrounding the tragic experiences of Polish deportees at the hands of the Soviets specifically from the Kresy region. On their website, you can listen to accounts of events from many years ago from the survivors themselves. The mission of the foundation is to document as much firsthand history before the stories are no longer remembered by anyone. The conference began on a fitting date, September 17, which commemorated the 75th anniversary of the Soviet invasion of Poland in 1939.

Commemoration of the Soviet invasion, Sept. 17, 1939, takes place every year in Warsaw at the sculpture constructed to honor those who were victimized. Conference attendees gather for this solemn commemoration.

I was excited to attend because it gave me the opportunity to hear stories of what the survivors experienced and put a face to what my parents and dad's family went through as a result of the Soviet deportations and imprisonments. The survivors who attended are elderly now but were children of all ages back in 1940 and 1941. Many traveled from their homes in South Africa, India, Australia, New Zealand, England, Scotland, and the United States to attend this conference. The second generation attendees were like me; there because they needed to know more about their families' exile experiences. I found that I shared a bond with these people. Many of us were researching our parents' stories, trying to reach some clarity on an ugly past. Some even traveled to Ukraine and Belarus after the conference to retrace deceased family members' steps and visit areas that used to be their families' villages in order to gather information. The child survivors of Siberia and those of the second-generation shared stories that were a wealth of information about their own experiences or those of their relatives. Several have either written books or were in the midst of writing, while others were there simply to stay connected with their history and the work of the foundation, which has been active since 2007.

It became clear to me, after initially having doubts, that I belonged at this conference. At the conference, young and old attendees were given the opportunity to share their stories. We saw and discussed a current documentary about Polish and Ukrainian citizens reconciling their history in a Ukrainian village, which in 1943, had experienced the mass murder of hundreds of Poles. This made me think about forgiveness since there was a great deal of anger and hostility in mom's attitude toward the Ukrainians because of my grandmother's murder. We took a tour of the temporary museum honoring the victims of the Katyń Massacre and I was able to see items collected from exhumations and excavations from the massacre sites. We also heard a lecture on the Molotov-Ribbentrop Pact, the German-Soviet Pact of 1939, describing the implications of the two evil war machines whose collective objectives set World War II into motion. I quickly realized that my family was directly impacted by all of these events: my mother's arrest and prison sentence, my dad's attempt to defend his country in 1939 and subsequent arrest and prison sentence, my grandparents' and aunt's deportation to Kazakhstan, my grandmother's murder by Ukrainian Nationalists, and my aunt's husband's murder in Katyń.

My family was touched by each of these historic events which involved eastern Poland, the Kresy, in their attempt to survive the war.

At the Katyń Museum, I was even able to find Adam's (my aunt's husband) name on the rolls of the murdered. The permanent Katyń Museum was dedicated the following year in September 2015 in time for the 76th anniversary of the Soviet Invasion and to commemorate the 75th anniversary of the massacre.

Letters from the Box in the Attic

The conference brought into focus an absolute connection of the stories from my past, the books I have read, the research I have done, to the hundreds of old letters written by my parents and their family, to history. During the letter translation phase of this project, I felt a keen connection to my mother, as if I were there with her during the trying times, as I attempted to read between the lines and understand what she was actually feeling. My parents' letters, written in their youth, revealed some of their innermost secrets, vulnerabilities, struggles, and fears which they shared with each other and their family. But the conference itself provided me with a certain pride, the joy of being Polish, a sense that I belonged in Poland when visiting, and not just as a tourist. I felt family roots and historical ties.

The following year, I also went back to Poland, but first went to visit Ewa and Jacek in their home in Opole, Poland and then took the train to Warsaw. There was another conference in Warsaw with the opening of the permanent Katyń Museum. It was planned to be in conjunction with the remembrance of the Soviet Invasion on September 17 once again. There was a memorial ceremony in Warsaw where streets were blocked off and large crowds attended; current military were in full dress uniform, many carrying large wreaths, like those laid at gravesites. This was a touching ceremony and I am proud to have now witnessed it twice. The conference again had an agenda of speakers, but the highlight was going to the soft opening of the permanent Katyń Museum.

My fascination with Katyń grew to an expanded and more meaningful scale as the curator spoke to us while giving a personal tour explaining at great length the excavations. The many ordinary, mundane relics are very interesting to see, including combs, toothbrushes, wedding rings, parts of uniforms including dog tags, and many hand-carved miniature chess sets which the prisoners created to pass the time. They all survived seventy-five years.

Because of my growing love for the Polish capital, I arranged to stay a few extra days in Warsaw to be able to experience the city and found myself sitting at a few outdoor cafes. There is a lovely street in Warsaw called Nowy Świat, which means new world.

It is a very busy street with many shops and restaurants which then leads north to the Old Town section of Warsaw. One warm late afternoon, I was delighted to be sitting at a café, sipping a glass of wine, watching the hustle and bustle as commuters and people of all generations strolled by. Many cars and buses filled the street. My imagination took me back to the summer of 1939 when so many young people, living and working in Warsaw, also would step out to the cafes and restaurants after work or gathered with family or friends on weekends, sipping wine at outdoor cafes, probably thinking about their futures. How innocent life can be in one moment and be turned upside down the next! I think of how my own adult children experience their downtime socializing with friends and family, and then cringe when I think of what my mother's generation experienced in the summer of 1939. They had to wonder what would be on the horizon next, not even fathoming what could actually happen. The optimism that many young people share is a survival tactic all its own.

I left a few days later with the hope of returning again the following year as the country and the city of Warsaw were becoming near and dear to my heart. The following year, I was not able to attend the conference because of work obligations, but there was a special treat in store for me and for my Polish cousins. My youngest child, my daughter Samantha, would join me for a trip to Poland that fall but a month after the conference. Earlier in 2016, she had applied for a grant from her company who offered their employees the opportunity to experience a trip or an activity that they otherwise would not or could not do because of time and/or money constraints.

She won the highest grant, but it needed to be used that calendar year and it was her preference to go to Poland. She expressed a desire to learn more about her Polish heritage and about her grandmother. I was so touched by this. We scheduled the trip for October and spent three days in Opole, Poland for her to meet her Polish cousins and four days in Warsaw.

Samantha began the grant application by writing, "When I was a kid, I always remember my grandmother being the most loving, caring person and yet the strangest. She had a funny accent, kept everything, would take rolls from restaurants, hated fish heads, always feared she would get lost and (she) worried about everything." How observant of Sammy. Her submission went on to say that she would use the grant money to visit her ancestral land, have time to reflect on the past, and use her newfound knowledge to appreciate the life she lives now because of the amazing people in her life, her family.

Samantha in Opole with Ewa and Jacek, our cousins—October 2016.

After the trip, she reported on two primary takeaways. The first is the unbelievable notion that Poles, her grandparents, had put their lives and family on the line to defend their country and never go back to it. This amazed her. "Never to see their family again because they were too scared of the Soviets to return! This I just cannot imagine," she went on to say. While visiting the cousins, she formulated the other takeaway which was by observing Ewa and me, sitting across the dining room table from one another at Ewa's home in Opole. There we were with our similarities and our differences. We were basically the same age, and both proud of our heritage, sharing and relating to stories of our parents' war experiences. But the differences were profound, all because of decisions that were made following the war.

Samantha found it fascinating that because her grandparents chose not to return to Poland, the outcome of that decision was that I would be raised in the United States, exposed to and able to embrace the American Dream. Meanwhile, Ewa grew up with her family close by but had to live under repressive Communism. Ewa spoke about the shortages, the long ration lines, neighbors telling on neighbors. "It's just amazing how one decision can affect so much and how the political environment of a nation can make such a huge impact on one's life. We are blessed to have the freedoms that we have," she wrote.

Samantha visiting the grave of her great-grandmother and great aunt.

I can't help but be proud of my daughter! Her grandmother would have been beaming with pride just knowing that Samantha wanted to visit Poland, and more so for taking the time and being willing to meet her cousins. Samantha did this without speaking the language. I had to use my limited language skills to translate all the conversations back and forth, like a ping pong ball, going from one person to the next, translating Polish and English. I have one more trip planned but hope to return in subsequent years as well. This upcoming trip is planned for the fall of 2018 and will be my fourth trip. I'm excited to take my husband Alan to meet the cousins and then to show him Warsaw. I will definitely need to keep my Polish language skills as sharp as possible.

Final Thoughts

Emma never stopped being proud of her Polish heritage for even a day of her life, but she also needed to integrate into American society. She was always so Polish in an Anglo culture, which bothered me and sometimes embarrassed me when I was younger. Being a child, I was always trying to fit in. Because she was so proud of her heritage, she was true to who she was. My mother's early experiences were the focal point of her life, certainly when it was happening but later, those experiences became an integral part of her. Emma's early years influenced and shaped how she viewed the world. It was through that lens of pain, trauma, hope, and love that she lived a righteous life, a moral and just life. The pain from her past, the reason why she would break out in cold sweats at night or in a store, never allowed her to forgive the country that was responsible for the trauma. Added to those feelings of hatred was how she felt about the Ukrainian people who murdered her mother. These two countries, once one and the same, still had a stronghold on her emotionally. Some may say that the sins of the father should be forgiven, but in Emma's world, the Soviets, the Ukrainians, the Russians, a collective from past centuries to the present, are not to be trusted. Evil may be disguised by a coat of a different color, but beneath that coat, the same evil lurks and it is how she felt. History has shown why this is true, as history does have a way of repeating itself. I do not judge, because I honor and understand her feelings.

Despite all the hardship the Polish people have known, the souls of these people have remained strong. The strength and resilience of the Polish people which have been tested time and time again make me proud. During her young adulthood, that decade from the start of the war until Emma came to the United States, that time of trauma and uncertainty, was not just an interruption in her life; it was a seminal time in her earthly history, a period of time that forever defined who she was. Having known her and now having delved deeper into the remarkable influences of her past, I better understand the whys of her life.

I have grown from being a reluctant Pole to a person who is proud of her heritage. The pivotal realization occurred toward the end of my second trip to Warsaw. Spending those few extra days in Warsaw after one of the conferences, I was able to walk the streets and learn my way around the growing city. This made me feel like I belonged. On my way to the airport, the cab driver paid me a compliment. He said my Polish was quite good. He was kind and knew I was not native but nonetheless, I was flattered. It felt good to be a part of Warsaw, and all of Poland. Previously, this had been an unknown and strange feeling for me. From my arrival on the shores of the United States as a DP, a refugee from a resettlement program, to dealing with and understanding my mother's past as a Polish patriot, I believe that through this project, I have embraced who I am.

I am my mother's daughter, a Polish patriot.

Bibliography

Archival Collections:

Centralne Archiwum Wojskowe - Polish Military Service Records

Hoover Institution of War, Revolution, and Peace - General Anders Collection, Box 203, Folder 5

IPN - Instituta Pamięci Narodowej), Institute of Polish Remembrance

Ministry of Defense - APC Polish Historical Disclosures

Published Reference Material:

Anders, Władysław - *An Army in Exile: The Story of the Second Polish Corps.* London: MacMillan, 1949.

Davies, Norman - *Trail of Hope, The Anders Army, An Odyssey Across Three Continents.* Rosikon Press, 2015.

Gross, Jan T. - *Revolution from Abroad: The Soviet Conquest of Poland's Western Ukraine and Western Belorussia.* Princeton University Press, 2002

Kochanski, Halik - *The Eagle Unbowed, Poland and the Poles in the Second World War.* Harvard University Press, 2012.

Moorhouse, Roger - *Berlin at War,* Basic Books, a Member of the Perseus Books Group New York, 2010

Moorhouse, Rodger - *The Devils' Alliance, Hitler's Pact with Stalin, 1939-1941.* The Bodley Head, 2014.

Snyder, Timothy - *Bloodlands, Europe Between Hitler and Stalin.* Basic Books, 2010.

The Polish Museum of America, *General Władysław Anders and the 2nd Polish Corps in the Marche Region, Italy, 1944-1946,* Exhibit, April 25 - May 31,2008.

Digital and Video Sources:

The Battle of Monte Cassino.
http://www.historylearningsite.co.uk/
second battle monte cassino.htm.

Bingle, Jean C. - *Labor for Bread: The Exploitation of Polish Labor in the Soviet Union During World War II.* Dissertation submitted to The Eberly College of Arts and Sciences at West Virginia University, 1999.

Creation of the Second Polish Corps.
http://www.polishgreatness.com/index.html

Fischer, Benjamin B., *The Katyń Controversy: Stalin's Killing Field* - Central Intelligence Agency. https://www.cia.gov/library/center-for-the-study-of-intelligence/csi.../art6.htm.

Gross, Jan T. - *Russian Rule in Poland, 1939-1941.* Yale University, contractor, 1983. Final report to National Council for Soviet and East European Research Contract # 620-6.

History of Akmolinsk-Kartaly Railway Construction (1939-1945).
http://e-history.kz/en/contents/view/1469.

Gulag.
http://en.wikipedia.org/wiki/Gulag.

The Italian Campaign of World War 2.
http://custermen.com/ItalyWW2/History.htm.

This Day in History.
www.history.com/this-day-in-history/germans-invade-poland

Iran and the Polish Exodus from Russia 1942.
http://www.parstimes.com/history/polish refugees/exodus russia.html

Monte Cassino, The Historical Eye.
http://historicaleye.WorldWar2/monte-cassino.html.

Naimark, Norman - Stanford News http://news.stanford.edu/2010/09/23/naimark-stalin-genocide-092310/

The Phony War.
https://en.m.wikipedia.org/wiki/Phoney War

Polish Second Corp.
https://www.revolvy.com/topic/Polish%20II%20Corps&itemtype=topic

Typhus. http://www.medicinenet.com/typhus/page2.htm.
Wesolowshki, Dr. Zdzislaw P, Colonel, South Carolina State Guard, (Reserve) -

The Polish Monte Cassino Cross. http://www.virtuti.com/order/articles/cassino.html.

Wajda, Andrzej and Nowakowski, Przemysław - *Katyń*, Polish Film, 2007.

Wright, Jagna and Naszynska, Aneta - *Forgotten Odyssey*, Documentary Film, 2001.

About the Author

Barbara Serbinski Sipe is a first-generation Polish immigrant from a refugee resettlement camp in Great Britain. Barbara grew up loving history and this love became a passion especially when it involved World War II and specifically the European conflict. Ignited by the love of European history, the project, Letters from the Box in the Attic, a Story of Courage, Survival, and Love is factually based on letters and documents discovered in the attic of her mother.

Historical perspective is preserved when placing her mother's letters and experiences into this narrative. Understanding why things happen in life and how they affect life is just as important as the events themselves. This is therefore the reason behind the extensive research and introspection found in this book.

Letters from the Box in the Attic is told by her daughter, Barbara, tracing her mother's journey from the Soviet invasion of Poland to Soviet prison cells and eventual release from a Siberian labor camp. The journey continues through the deserts of the Middle East, to Italy, and on the shores of Great Britain.

www.ingramcontent.com/pod-product-compliance
Lightning Source LLC
Chambersburg PA
CBHW021441070526
44577CB00002B/234